"OUR NAME IS PETER"

An Anthology of Key Teachings
of
Pope Paul VI

Compiled by

Sean O'Reilly, M.D., F.R.C.P.

FRANCISCAN HERALD PRESS
1434 West 51st Street
Chicago, Illinois 60609

Our Name Is Peter by Sean O'Reilly. Copyright © 1977 by Franciscan Herald Press, 1434 W. 51st Street, Chicago, Illinois 60609. Made in the United States of America. All rights reserved.

Library of Congress Cataloging in Publication Data:

Main entry under title:

Our name is Peter.

   1. Papacy—Addresses, essays, lectures.
2. Paulus VI, Pope, 1897-   —Addresses, essays, lectures. I. O'Reilly, Sean, 1922-
BX955.2.095   262'.13'0924   77-380
ISBN 0-8199-0666-2

NIHIL OBSTAT:
   Mark Hegener O.F.M.
   Censor Librorum

IMPRIMATUR:
   ✠ Most Rev. Thomas J. Welsh
   Bishop of Arlington

November 4, 1976

MADE IN THE UNITED STATES OF AMERICA

Dedication

To His Holiness Pope Paul VI on the occasion of his eightieth birthday, the 56th of his priesthood and the 14th of his supreme pontificate, with humble heartfelt gratitude and filial love.

Foreword

Some might ask: with what competence does Dr. Sean O'Reilly, a neurologist, write a theological essay? Where did he study biblical criticism, hermeneutics, theological methodology?

Doctor O'Reilly is not a biblical scholar. He is not a theologian. He is not a philosopher. This book is not a theological essay.

It is an account: an account of the hope that he has (cf. 1 Peter 3,15). Doctor O'Reilly is a man of faith, fiercely devoted to the Catholic Church and profoundly loyal to her heritage. In addition, he has acquired great experience advising many who have been deeply troubled by the changes in the Church in the last decade. Doctor O'Reilly is very sensitive to their anxieties and concerns, and has spent much time in helping them understand the renewal of the Church as the Second Vatican Council called for it. This must be kept in mind when reading this book.

In a word, then, Doctor O'Reilly is that layman of whom the Second Vatican Council declared: "every lay person, through those gifts given to him, is at once the witness and the living instrument of the mission of the Church itself 'according to the measure of Christ's bestowal' (Eph. 4, 7)" (Lumen Gentium, 33).

Readers of this book will be grateful to Doctor O'Reilly

for giving to us a magnificent compendium of the teaching of Pope Paul VI. Throughout the book we hear the voice of the Holy Father, a pastor who experiences in his person the sufferings and joys of the Church of today; an evangelist endowed with a prophetic understanding of the world in which we live; an apostle consumed by the zeal to offer to modern humanity the liberating message of the gospel and the service of the Church in the task of constructing, out of the immense cultural changes of the present time, what he has called the "civilization of love." Doctor O'Reilly's book will help many take heart in the secure conviction that the Apostle Peter is with us, confirming his brethren in the faith.

William Cardinal Baum
Archbishop of Washington

Feast of the Presentation of Our Lord
February 2, 1977

Preface

"I will look after my sheep, says the Lord, and I will raise up one shepherd who will pasture them." (Ezekiel 34:11, 23-24) These words of the prophet Ezekiel foretell the essential details of God's salvation plan: He will send His own Divine Son among men to be the Good Shepherd, the One Shepherd. When in the fullness of time decreed by the Father, Christ Our Lord walked with His disciples and taught the crowds who followed Him, the imagery of Ezekiel was frequently on His lips, the imagery of the good shepherd who knows His sheep and for whom He will lay down His life.

The Church which He established was to be a shepherd, and when He chose the one whom He wished to be in charge, His commission to Peter was expressed in the same imagery: "Feed my lambs, feed my lambs, feed my sheep," He told the Apostle.

This imagery has seldom left the mind of the Church since then. She applies it to Herself, to Her Popes, to Her bishops and priests, and to all of us Her faithful flock. It is significant, surely, that She has used the very words of Ezekiel as the entrance antiphon for the memorial Mass of St. Ambrose. For it was Ambrose who said, 'Ubi Petrus ibi Ecclesia,' 'Where Peter is there is the Church.' And surely it is no accident of history that Pope Paul VI occupied the see of St.

Ambrose in Milan when he was elected as the chief shepherd of the flock of Christ. Only too well in the 14 years of his pontificate has he experienced the full force and significance of this biblical and ecclesiastical imagery—shepherd, flock, wolves! This book tries to present some of the crucial teachings of Pope Paul in his own words, in the context of some essential historical background and the author's reflections on those teachings. It is an attempt to grasp the manifest mind and will of the Vicar of Christ on earth as he has expressed it so often and so well.

Two motives led to its publication. One is a hope, the other is a prayer—the hope, that others may be led to read and reflect on the teachings of this great Pope; the prayer, that he may in his sufferings for Our Lord and the Church derive some consolation from it.

Sean O'Reilly
McLean, Virginia

Feast of St. Ambrose
Eve of the Feast of the
    Immaculate Conception
7th December 1976

Acknowledgements

I wish to express my gratitude and appreciation to my wife, Anne, for her constructive, critical, and intuitive comments; to my oldest daughter, Anne Mary, for patiently typing and re-typing most of the manuscript; to a former research associate, Miss Mary Oswald, of San Francisco, for material assistance; to Bishop Thomas J. Welsh of Arlington for his official assurance that the book is free of doctrinal error so far as the author's interpretation of the meaning of Pope Paul's teachings are concerned; and last, though not least, I thank His Eminence Cardinal Baum for his gracious agreement to write a foreword.

Contents

1. The Pope as Teacher

It would seem unnecessary to justify the legitimate claims of the supreme pastor of the Church, the pope, but seldom before has the teaching authority of the Holy Father been subject to such attacks from outside the Church, and even from within it by those who still claim to be Catholics. It is worthwhile, therefore, to review the essential historical and doctrinal background of our acceptance of the supreme teaching authority of Pope Paul VI.

The History

Everyone remembers St. Matthew's account of the occasion on which our Lord declared Peter the future cornerstone, indeed the very foundation, on which his Church was to be built. On their way to Caesarea Philippi, he asked his disciples, "Who is the Son of Man in the eyes of the public?" A curious question, at first sight, to which he got a number of answers: John the Baptist, Elias, Jeremias, one of the prophets. He persisted, "But who do *you* say that I am?" Simon Peter answered, "You are the Christ, the Son of the Living God!"

Then Jesus said, "Blessed are you, Simon Bar-Jona, for flesh and blood has not revealed this to you, but my Father in heaven. And I say to you: you are Peter [the rock], and upon this rock I will build my Church, and the gates of hell shall not prevail against it. And I will give you the keys of the kingdom of heaven; and whatever you shall bind on earth shall be bound in heaven, and whatever you shall loose on earth shall be loosed in heaven."

These words are clear and unmistakable in promising the primacy to Peter. And so they were understood by all— clearly. It is evident in all the gospels and in the Acts of the Apostles that Peter was the first in rank among the apostles, outranking even "the disciple whom Jesus loved," in whose gospel we read the account of the actual conferring on Peter, by our divine Lord, of His commission as the supreme pastor and teacher of his Church.

We do well to note the qualification he demanded of Peter before giving him this commission, "Simon, son of John, do you love me more than these do?" Three times he repeated this fundamental question, and in answer to Peter's repeated avowals he commanded him: "Feed my lambs, feed my lambs, feed my sheep." In other words, he demanded of Peter a primacy of love before conferring on him the pastoral primacy.

We also recall St. Luke's account of the Last Supper, after which our Lord said, "Simon, Simon, behold—Satan has desired to have you, that he may sift you as wheat. But I have prayed for you, that your faith may not fail, and do you strengthen your brethren once you have been converted."

The future history of the Church, indeed of all mankind, is summed up in those words of our Lord. For the eye of faith sees that the really important, the seminal events in human history since that time have been Satan's constant attempts to sift Peter's successors like wheat, and the constantly recurring miracle of his failure to get the pope to teach formal heresy.

In reviewing the 2,000-year history of the Catholic Church, it is evident there were periods, some of them very lengthy, when nothing was said formally or publicly about the papal primacy, but as Cardinal Newman so aptly said, "Silence [about a doctrine] at a certain period implies, not that it was not then held, but that it was not questioned" (*The Development of Christian Doctrine*, p. 401). The primacy of Peter

and his successors in the see of Rome was affirmed publicly
and frequently by the early fathers of the Church, such as
St. Irenaeus, St. Ignatius of Antioch, St. Cyprian of Carthage,
St. Augustine. It was challenged from time to time, especially with the rise of Arianism, so it is not surprising to find
that the first conciliar promulgation of the primacy was made
in 381, fifty-six years after Nicea, at the second general council of the Church (the First Council of Constantinople).

The most noteworthy and emphatic reaffirmation of the
primacy and supreme authority of the pope, however, was
made at the third general council, that of Ephesus (431).
The stage had been set for it by the fact that the council had
begun *before* the three papal legates arrived, and had already
condemned, excommunicated, and deposed Nestorius. When
the legates arrived, the council reassembled and the letter of
Pope St. Celestine I, condemning Nestorius' teaching, was
read. The council members cried out as one: "Celestine is the
guardian of the faith; Celestine agrees with the council!"

Their acclamations were cut short by one of the papal legates, who pointed out that Celestine's letter had said it was
the council's business to agree with *him*, and carry out what
he, at Rome, had decided should be done.

Another legate said, "The members have joined themselves
to the Head," and addressing the presiding prelate directly,
he added, "for Your Beatitude is not ignorant that the Head
of the whole Faith, and furthermore of the Apostles, is the
Blessed Apostle Peter."

As if this were not enough, at the next day's session the
same legate, having reviewed the official record of the council's first session (which had been held three weeks before the
papal legates arrived), declared that the judgment to con-
demn Nestorius had been made "canonically and in accordance with ecclesiastical learning," and it was confirmed "con-
formably with the instructions of the most Holy Pope, Celestine." In the speech that followed, he made an affirmation
of immense importance:

> No one doubts, nay it is a thing known for centuries,
> that the Holy and most Blessed Peter, the Prince and
> Head of the Apostles, the Pillar of the Faith and the

> Foundation on which the Catholic Church is built, re-
> ceived from Our Lord Jesus Christ, the Savior and
> Redeemer of the Human Race, the Keys of the Kingdom,
> and that to Him there was given the power of binding and
> of loosing from Sin; Who down to this day, and forever-
> more, lives and exercises judgment in His Successors.

So we are not surprised to find that twenty years later, at the Council of Chalcedon (451), concerned with the Monophysite heresy (which held that our Lord has only one nature, the divine nature), the decisive document was the tome of Pope St. Leo I (the letter he wrote to the bishop of Constantinople, Flavian). In it the pope set out authoritatively that which the Catholic Church universally believes and teaches about the mystery of the incarnation of our Lord. And at the sixth general council in 680 (the Third Council of Constantinople) the doctrine of the role of the pope in a general council was set out more completely and explicitly than ever.

Pope Agatho wrote a letter to the council, addressed to the emperor, Constantine IV, which was an authoritative statement of the traditional faith, modeled on the tome of Pope St. Leo. In this letter the pope told the emperor, and through him the council fathers, that the function of his legates was to explain what the Roman Church teaches. They did not come as learned theologians, (*periti*, we would call them nowadays) "but as bringing testimony of what is believed; they are charged to state the tradition of this Apostolic See, as it has been taught by our Apostolic predecessors; and they have been commanded not to presume to add or take away or change anything."

After the statement of belief or creed, he said that "this is the true and undefiled profession of the Christian religion, which no human cleverness invented, but which the Holy Ghost taught by the Prince of the Apostles. This is the firm and irreprehensible doctrine of the Apostles."

We read in the history of the council that the pope's letter was received with acclamation by the fathers, who shouted, "It is Peter who is speaking through Agatho!"

One hundred years or so later, we read of Charlemagne's striking reaffirmation of this traditional doctrine of the supremacy of the papal teaching: "Whenever a dispute arises about matters of belief, we must consult the Holy, Roman, Catholic and Apostolic Church, which is set in authority over the other churches."

By contrast, a secular emperor of a different stripe in the thirteenth century, Frederick II, emperor of Germany, tried to rouse the cardinals of the Sacred College against Pope Gregory IX. Frederick appealed his excommunication by Gregory to the cardinals, telling them that the pope was no more than a kind of chairman of their college, but to no avail.

The First Council of Lyons (1245), the thirteenth general council, called by Gregory's successor, Innocent IV, issued a bull of excommunication and deposition against Frederick, the beginning of the end for the house of Hohenstaufen. Twenty-nine years later, the fourteenth general council, the Second Council of Lyons (1274), reaffirmed the doctrine of the primacy of the Roman see. The first two sentences of the reaffirmation were used by the fathers of the First Vatican Council (1870) in their definition of the infallibility of the pope's *ex cathedra* decisions.

But the road ahead was extremely rocky for the papal primacy and the magisterium, despite the repeated affirmations. Two events stand out in the history of those stormy centuries, after the decline and destruction of medieval Christendom, and the first was the sixteenth general council, the Council of Constance (1414–18), one of the great turning points in the history of the Church. Thereafter things were never again the same in one very important matter: the pope's right to rule the whole Church as its earthly master— a right that had been reaffirmed time and again and painfully established as an unquestioned general belief, as we have seen. The mischief was wrought by a decree of the council, *Sacrosancta*, which declared:

> This Holy Council of Constance . . . declares, in the first place, that lawfully come together in the Holy Spirit, being a General Council and representing the Catholic Church, it holds an authority directly [derived] from Christ, which authority everyone, of whatever status or dignity, even the Pope, is bound to obey in those matters concerning the Faith, the extirpation of the said Schism

> [the Great Schism of the West], and the reformation of
> the Church in Head and members.

This was a resounding manifesto of antipapalism, destined to agitate the Church for centuries, and manifested in many ways. It is understandable why it was made, given the sorry state of the papacy at the time. There were three "popes": an Italian, John XXIII, who had convened the council; a Frenchman, Gregory XII; and a Spaniard, Benedict XIII. The council proceeded to depose two of them, accepted the resignation of the third, and elected a pope of its own, Martin V, whereupon one of those providential interventions, so common in the history of the Church, occurred. Of all the decrees put out by the council, only the seven published after Martin V's election received papal approval, and *Sacrosancta* was not one of them.

It is quite clear that most decrees of the Council of Constance were not ratified by the pope and hence were not binding. But the council that followed Constance, that began at Basel in 1431, renewed the decrees on the general council's superiority to the pope, Martin V's successor, Eugene IV. He in turn notified the council that the pope is nonetheless its superior, and six years after it began he denounced the council, transferred it to Ferrara, and then to Florence (in 1439), when he declared null and void the rebellious decrees, including *Sacrosancta*, and excommunicated the rump council that had persisted at Basel. This was a clear-cut victory for papal primacy, which was reaffirmed in no uncertain terms at the eighteenth general council in 1512, the Fifth Lateran Council, which accepted and approved Pope Leo X's bull *Pastor Aeternus*. This bull reaffirmed that the reigning pope alone can call a general council, and can adjourn or dissolve it. The reminder that the Roman see is sovereign in the Church was driven home by a renewal, in 1302, of Pope Boniface VIII's famous bull *Unam Sanctam*.

This is all the more surprising when we recall the character of Pope Leo X, the Medici pope, who was a "gilded bufferfly," addicted to pleasure, especially music, art, and hunting and, as he himself admitted, devoid of theological knowledge. But it was this same Leo X who, when presented with a heretical document and under pressure to sign it, exclaimed "*Non possumus!* We cannot!" The victory was short-lived, however; the Fifth Lateran Council ended just seven months before Luther's defiance, his theses against indulgences (1517).

Thus began the second serious assault on papal supremacy, the Protestant "Reformation." It is essential to realize that Luther's revolt, almost from the beginning, was explicitly directed against the pope's essential claim that he is the ruler of the entire Church. This is clear from the two pamphlets Luther wrote in 1520. In one of them he denounced the papacy as a vast financial enterprise which was plundering Germany—a charge sure to popularize him immediately with the mercenary and rapacious German princes who were casting greedy eyes on Church property. The second pamphlet showed how the popes had systematically "corrupted" Christian teaching for 1,000 years. So he called on the German princes to destroy the papacy, and in a bonfire on the town dunghill at Wittenberg burned not only the bull *Exsurge Domine*, which condemned him, but the entire collection of papal laws that binds the whole Church.

In light of this, it is at first sight astonishing to realize that the Council of Trent, summoned twenty-five years later to restate Catholic beliefs in opposition to the Protestant errors, and to reform Catholic life, did not directly address itself to reaffirmation of the doctrine of papal primacy and papal authority. One wonders if God, in his providential wisdom, did not first wish to provide a practical demonstration of the necessity of a supreme ruler, a visible head for his mystical body, the Church—which of course he did provide, in the persons of Pope Paul IV, who patiently and prudently brought the council to a close, setting up a permanent commission of cardinals to settle authoritatively all questions of interpretation of the decrees of Trent, and Pope St. Pius V, who set to work to implement the decrees. It is evident, however successful Trent was in inaugurating and underpinning the true reformation, that attacks on the papacy and doubts about its teaching and juridical supremacy continued, not only among the Protestant factions but within the Church itself. Witness the Gallican errors and the rise of Modernism.

When the proposal to define the doctrine of papal supremacy and infallibility was broached at the First Vatican Council (1869–70), it met significant opposition, not only on grounds that it was inopportune but also that it was nondefinable. There were some who held it simply was not true. However, we know it was defined *de fide*, and the ghost of the decree *Sacrosancta* of the Council of Constance was finally and officially laid.

The teachings of Vatican I in this defined doctrine, as expressed in the decree *Pastor Aeternus*, were amplified, developed, and reaffirmed in the documents of Vatican II. Both Vatican councils provided an emphatic, infallible reaffirmation of what has always been taught by the Holy See. Let us turn, then, to the doctrinal content of these teachings.

Papal Primacy and Papal Infallibility

Before we present the details of the doctrines defined in the decree *Pastor Aeternus*, solemnly promulgated by Pope Pius IX after the final vote of the First Vatican Council, let us recall that the Council of Trent made two pertinent preliminary definitions of doctrine:

> *Christ gave His Church a Hierarchical Constitution,* declaring: If anyone says there is not a hierarchy instituted by Divine Ordinance in the Catholic Church, let him be anathema [D. 966].

> *The powers bestowed on the Apostles have descended to the Bishops* [D. 960].

These two propositions are therefore *de fide definita*, and had been held and taught from the earliest times.

Pastor Aeternus methodically set out the following defined doctrines on the primacy and infallibility of the pope.

1. Christ appointed the Apostle Peter to be the first of all the Apostles and to be the visible head of the whole Church, by appointing him immediately and personally to the primacy of jurisdiction.

2. According to Christ's ordinance, Peter is to have suc-

cessors in his primacy over the whole Church and for all time.

3. The successors of Peter in the primacy are the bishops of Rome.

The second and third definitions state the fact of the primacy of jurisdiction of the pope. The fourth statement is concerned with the *nature* of the papal primacy:

4. *"The Pope possesses full and supreme power of jurisdiction over the whole Church, not merely in matters of faith and morals, but also in Church discipline and in the government of the Church."*

This primatial power is

a) *A true power of jurisdiction*, that is, a true governing power, and embraces the full power of legislation, executive action, and jurisdiction.

b) *A universal power*, that is, extending personally to all the bishops, pastors, and all members of the Church, collectively and individually. It covers both the teaching office and the pastoral office.

c) *A supreme power*, that is, no one bishop or all the bishops collectively (excluding the pope) have greater or equally great power.

d) *A full and personal power*, that is, the pope can rule independently, without the concurrence of the other bishops or the rest of the Church.

e) *An ordinary power*, that is, it is connected with the office and is not delegated from some other jurisdiction, that is, the College of Cardinals or the bishops of a council. Therefore, the pope can exercise it at any time and not merely in exceptional cases.

f) *An episcopal power*, that is, the pope is as much a universal bishop of the whole Church as he is bishop of his diocese in Rome.

g) *An immediate power*, that is, the pope needs no intermediary; he can exercise his power directly over the bishops and the faithful of the whole Church.

5. The First Vatican Council went further than the above definitions of the primacy of jurisdiction of the pope. It also defined as *de fide* the dogma that the pope is infallible when he speaks *ex cathedra.*

In the historical survey, reference was made to the reaffirmation by the Second General Council of Lyons in the thirteenth century of the doctrine of the primacy of the Roman see. The testimony of this council was used in the First Vatican Council's definition of papal infallibility and reads as follows:

> This same Holy Roman Church itself has, over the whole Catholic Church, the supreme and full primacy and sovereign authority; which, it humbly and truthfully recalls to mind, the Roman Church received from the Lord Himself, with all fullness of power, through Blessed Peter, the chief and the head of the Apostles, of whom the Bishop of Rome is successor.
>
> And as, before all else, that Church is bound to protect the true belief, so it is that whenever disputes arise about the Faith, they must be decided by the judgment of that Church.

Against the background of that testimony, it is easy to see the development of doctrine in the Vatican I definition. The doctrine of the teaching primacy of the Holy See, already affirmed so many times, *in its essence implied infallibility*, and the Vatican I definition simply made explicit what was already implicit. It is essential that we understand the definition, which is as follows:

> The Roman Pontiff, when he speaks *ex cathedra*— that is, when in discharge of the office of Pastor and Doctor of all Christians, by virtue of his supreme apostolic authority, he defines a doctrine regarding faith or morals to be held by the universal Church—by the Divine assistance promised to him in Blessed Peter, is possessed of that infallibility with which the Divine Redeemer willed that His Church should be endowed in defining doctrine regarding faith or morals; and therefore such definitions of the Roman Pontiff are irreformable of themselves, and not in virtue of the consent of the Church.

It is important to understand precisely what is defined, namely, the personal infallibility of the reigning, lawfully elected pope when he speaks *ex cathedra*, that is, with the full weight of his supreme apostolic authority as pastor and teacher of *all* the Church, on a matter of faith or morals, with the intention, either explicit in the formulation or manifest by the circumstances, that the teaching so promulgated is to be believed and practiced by all the faithful.

The infallibility of the Church was not explicitly defined, though it is *implied*, in the definition of papal infallibility which we have just read. To repeat the essential pertinent statement: "The Roman Pontiff, when he speaks *ex cathedra* . . . is possessed of that infallibility *with which the Divine Redeemer willed that His Church should be endowed* for defining doctrine regarding faith or morals."

We should add, though it is scarcely necessary, that no individual bishop or group of bishops, no theologian or body of theologians, no group of Catholics, clerical or lay, is infallible. The entire College of Bishops, in unity with the pope, is infallible, *ex ordinario magisterio*, as is said, when it promulgates or teaches the same body of doctrine on faith or morals. It is infallible, *ex extraordinario magisterio*, when it defines a doctrine or issues solemn decrees on matters of faith and morals in a lawful general council. The latter must fulfill the following norms: (i) all the ruling bishops of the world must be invited, (ii) a representative number of those invited must attend, (iii) the pope must issue the convocation, or at least invest the assembly with his authority, (iv) the assembly must be presided over by the pope or his personal representatives, and (v) the decrees must be approved and ratified by the pope.

Although no new dogmas were defined by the Second Vatican Council, it behooves us to examine carefully the documents of the council to see what is said about the primacy of jurisdiction and teaching and the infallibility of the pope.

In the very first chapter of *Lumen Gentium*, the dogmatic constitution on the Church, we read:

> After His Resurrection our Savior handed her [the Church] over to Peter to be shepherded, commissioning him and the other Apostles to propagate and govern her. Her He erected for all ages as "the pillar and mainstay" of the truth. This Church . . . subsists in the Catholic

> Church, which is governed by the successor of Peter and by the Bishops in union with that successor. [*L.G.*, 1:8]

Then, in chapter 3, the council, in its own words,

> following in the footsteps of the First Vatican Council, teaches and declares with that Council that Jesus Christ, the eternal Shepherd, established His Holy Church by sending forth the Apostles as He Himself had been sent by the Father. He willed that their successors, namely the Bishops, should be shepherds in His Church even to the consummation of the world.
>
> In order that the episcopate itself might be one and undivided, He placed Blessed Peter over the other Apostles, and instituted in him a permanent and visible source and foundation of unity of faith and fellowship.
>
> And all this teaching about the institution, the perpetuity, the force and reason for the sacred primacy of the Roman Pontiff and of his infallible teaching authority, this sacred synod again proposes to be firmly believed by all the faithful. [*L.G.*, 3:18]

What could be clearer and more forceful? Section 22 of chapter 3, for instance, says:

> Just as, by the Lord's will, St. Peter and the other Apostles constituted one apostolic College, so in a similar way the Roman Pontiff as the successor of Peter, and the Bishops as the successors of the Apostles are joined together . . . but the college or body of Bishops has no authority unless it is simultaneously conceived of in terms of its head, the Roman Pontiff, Peter's successor, and without any lessening of his power of primacy over all, pastors as well as the general faithful. For in virtue of his office, that is, as Vicar of Christ and Pastor of the whole Church, the Roman Pontiff has full, supreme, and universal power over the Church. And he can always exercise this power freely . . . together with its head, the Roman Pontiff, and never without this head, the episcopal order is the subject of supreme and full power over the universal Church. But this power can be exercised only with the consent of the Roman Pontiff. For Our Lord made Simon Peter alone the rock and keybearer of the Church (cf. Mt. 16:18–19), and appointed him shepherd of the whole flock (cf. Jn. 21:15ff.).

So much for the primacy of jurisdiction. It is obvious that Vatican II, no less than Vatican I, gives no comfort or support to the proponents of conciliar supremacy. Indeed, the entire controversy was put in proper perspective in the prefatory note of explanation that was ordered to be published with the constitution *Lumen Gentium* by Pope Paul himself. In this note the authentic norm of interpretation for chapter 3, from which we have just quoted, is set forth. In it we find these very important statements:

> For necessarily and always the College carries with it the idea of its head, who preserves intact in the College his role of vicar of Christ and shepherd of the universal Church. In other words, there is no distinction between the Roman Pontiff and the Bishops taken collectively, but between the Roman Pontiff by himself, and the Roman Pontiff together with the bishops. . . . The care of the whole flock of Christ has been entrusted to the supreme Pontiff. . . . The Roman Pontiff proceeds according to his own discretion, and in view of the welfare of the Church, in structuring, promoting, and endorsing any exercise of collegiality. . . . As supreme Pastor of the Church, the sovereign Pontiff can always exercise his authority as he chooses, as is demanded by his office itself.

And what about infallibility? Let us hear what *Lumen Gentium* has to say:

> This infallibility with which the Divine Redeemer willed His Church to be endowed in defining a doctrine of faith and morals extends as far as extends the deposit of Divine Revelation. . . . This is the infallibility which the Roman Pontiff, the head of the College of Bishops, enjoys in virtue of his office when, as the Supreme Shepherd and teacher of all the faithful, who confirms his brethren in their faith, he proclaims by a definitive act some doctrine of faith or morals. Therefore his definitions, of themselves, and not from the consent of the Church, are justly styled irreformable . . . therefore they need no approval of others, nor do they allow an appeal to any other judgment. [*L.G.*, 3:25]

There are many echoes of these forthright statements on papal primacy and infallibility in the rest of this fundamental dogmatic constitution on the Church and in the other documents of the council, for example, in the preface and chapter 1 of the decree on the bishops' pastoral office in the Church (*Christus Dominus*). They give the lie completely to those who would say Vatican II did away with the papal power—that it put the pope "in his place"! It did indeed put him in his place—his proper place, as supreme pontiff, vicar of

Christ, visible head of the mystical body, the people of God, and head of the College of Bishops.

Lumen Gentium made another very important statement, even more pertinent, in a real and practical sense, than all we have considered so far—for the pope seldom speaks *ex cathedra*. Speaking of the primary duty of bishops, that of preaching and teaching the faith, *Lumen Gentium* states categorically that the faithful are to accept their teaching and adhere to it with a religious assent of soul. It goes on to say:

> This religious submission of will and of mind must be shown in a special way to the teaching authority of the Roman Pontiff, even when he is not speaking ex cathedra. That is, it must be shown in such a way that his supreme magisterium is acknowledged with reverence, the judgments made by him are sincerely adhered to, according to his manifest mind and will. His mind and will in the matter may be known chiefly either from the character of the documents, from his frequent repetition of the same doctrine, or from his manner of speaking. [*L.G.,* 3:25]

Thus it can be clearly seen that, in practical terms of the life of the Church, it is only in this way that Christ's will for the unity of his flock can be realized. The pope is, in any age, "the visible source and foundation of unity of faith and fellowship."

2. Pope and Council

The week of May 5 through 12, 1527, bore witness to what looked to be the fulfillment of Luther's furious response to his excommunication: the unleashing of all the passion he could muster against the papacy. For in that week the Eternal City of Rome was sacked, not as in the past by pagan hordes but by a Christian army, mostly of German Lutherans, troops of the Catholic emperor Charles V, incited by a traitor Frenchman, the Constable de Bourbon. In the words of a diplomat at the papal court, "Hell is nothing to what happened then."

Pope Clement VII watched the nightmare spectacle from the Castel San Angelo, where he had taken refuge, and he had no option but to surrender and accept the harsh terms imposed: surrender of the Papal States, a huge ransom, etc. In his letter to Charles V, accepting these conditions, he wrote "We have nothing before our eyes but a corpse in shreds." "A corpse in shreds"! A completely apt description of the state of Christendom at that time.

Yet the groundswell of true reform and rebirth of the Church was already gaining momentum, built up by bishops such as Cardinal Ximenes in Spain and the very wonderful Bishop Giberti in Verona, many of whose regulations for his clergy were subsequently incorporated word for word in the canons of Trent. The old orders of religious were being or had been reformed—the Franciscans, Dominicans, Augustinians; and who would have thought that in just seven years Ignatius and his companions would bring into being the Society of Jesus?

All the prerequisites for a Catholic reformation were present. The moral and spiritual climate of the times demanded it. But one thing was lacking: the intervention of supreme authority, that of the pope. For almost a century, various popes had spoken out on the need for reform, even those whose pontificates seemed to document most clearly the necessity for reform. Even Alexander VI, the Borgia pope, summoned a Commission of Reform and directed it to produce a bill of reform, *Flatus Vocis*, but none was carried beyond tentative beginnings. Clement VII's words, "a corpse in shreds," seemed destined to become the epitaph on the tomb of the institutional Church.

The election of Clement's successor, Paul III must have daunted even the most optimistic of those who longed for reform and renewal of the Church, for he began his reign with the most flagrant nepotism, raising two of his grandsons, ages 16 and 14, to the College of Cardinals. An inauspicious beginning to what was to prove a momentous pontificate, for Paul III was destined by God to set in motion the entire apparatus of reform and to convoke the Council of Trent. In the bull he sent to that council, he gave a perfect summary of the situation when he became pope.

> In those days all was full of hatred and dissension. Princes were everywhere at loggerheads with one another, princes to whom God had entrusted government. The unity of the Christian name had been shattered by schism and heresy. The Turks were advancing on land and sea; Rhodes was lost, Hungary devastated; Italy, Austria and Slavonia were threatened. The Divine Wrath lay heavy on all us sinners.

God surely writes straight with crooked lines. This pope was characterologically and intellectually endowed to undertake a truly superhuman task: to convoke a council against all opposition, internal as well as external, after initiating the necessary curial reforms to ensure that the council would be effective. When, finally, the first session of the council opened on December 13, 1545, it was a tribute to his tenacity, his courage and sheer energy, no less than to his shrewd intelligence and sound judgment of men and means. No matter that he had to suspend it after three and one half years, with only one really satisfactory series of sessions. The die was cast.

The council did not resume its work until 1550, when Julius III was pope, but was again interrupted by political events, and was not reassembled until after the four-year pontificate of Paul IV, the "terrible" Cardinal Carafa, who carried on his own reform campaign, much of which produced excellent results, his main tools being the Inquisition and the Congregation of the Index, which he established. Finally, during the reign of Pius IV, the council was brought to completion.

So, despite the obvious and well-known moral weakness of Paul III and Pius IV, the great work of Trent was accomplished. Even Pius IV's nepotism turned up a *felix culpa.* One of his many nephews, who was made a cardinal and secretary of state at the age of 22, turned out to be one of the greatest saints of the age, "the pope's right eye" in the work of reform: St. Charles Borromeo. And, surely, saints were needed to implement the reform so masterfully blueprinted by the decrees and canons of the greatest council in the history of the Church.

God did not fail to provide what was needed. The first and most necessary blessing from God on the Council of Trent had been providing the fathers of the council and their consultors with the vision and the wisdom essential to the task of formulating all the essential dogmas of the faith, based on Scripture and tradition, with a clarity, force, and inclusiveness the Church had never previously possessed.

Each of the sixteen dogmatic decrees restated the *whole* doctrine in question. In form, each was a miniature theological treatise, but they were carefully *not* written in technical theological language. Each dogmatic decree included one or more canons which were short, summary condemnations of heresies, old and new, which contradicted the doctrine set forth in the decree in question. In addition, a number of disciplinary decrees were directed toward reform of the Church in its head and members; the pope was urged to appoint as cardinals only men of exceptional character and gifts, and only the very best and most suitable pastors as diocesan bishops. The bishops received a tremendous body of instruction and rules on their duties and functions, as did priests. The most significant decreed reform was the establishment of diocesan seminaries and prescription of the intellectual and spiritual formation to be provided in them. For the laity, the council ordered a catechism to be prepared, a work that began even before the close of the council. The council also indicated that three other books were fundamental and essential: a revised breviary, a new missal, and a new edition of the *Summa* of St. Thomas Aquinas.

The second essential intervention of divine providence in the enormous task of reform of the Church was to ensure that the popes who followed Pius IV and the Council of Trent understood their duty and were qualified to fulfill it. The third essential was to raise up a sufficient number of saints to ensure that the spirit and teachings of the council would be injected deep into the Catholic conscience.

Already, God had begun to make the latter blessing a reality. Seven years before Trent came to its final session, St. Ignatius of Loyola and St. Francis Xavier were already gone to their eternal reward. St. Francis Borgia was in the Society, which now numbered over 1,000 members. St. Charles Borromeo was 25 years old, a cardinal, secretary of state to his uncle Pope Pius IV, and archbishop of Milan, and soon to become the spearhead of reform in the episcopal college. For another 25-year-old man also, the die had been cast: St. John of the Cross had met St. Teresa of Avila, with such consequences for reform of the Church in Spain as could never have been predicted by their contemporaries. These of course were not all; few periods in the history of the Church were blessed with so many and such outstanding saints—a veritable galaxy.

Surely the providence of God was becoming manifest to his people, and surely there was no more striking manifestation of his loving care than the election of Michael Ghislieri, prefect of the Holy Office, as supreme pontiff to succeed Pope

Pius IV three years after the close of the Council of Trent. Pope Pius V, as he chose to be named, was not only a very great pope, he was also a saint. At the very first consistory that he called after his election, he delivered an allocution which set the tone and the theme of his pontificate. Its thrust and import were summarized in two sentences.

> We shall not paralyze the advance of heresy except by an operation proceeding from the heart of God. It is we, the light of the world, the salt of the earth, who must enlighten men's minds, enliven their hearts by the example of our holiness and our virtues.

Rome soon learned that these were no idle, pharisaical words. It became known that the new pontiff lived in the Vatican in a monastic cell, drank only water, and spent hours in prayer—meditating on the passion, prostrate before the Blessed Sacrament, or reciting his rosary. And soon he was to be seen, barefoot, going his rounds, carrying the monstrance or visiting the basilicas as a humble pilgrim. Such a pope had not been seen for centuries, and Rome did not know what to think. The simple faithful were delighted and wanted to erect a statue to him, but he would have none of it. There were many in the Curia and its clerical fringes who had trembled on his election, regarding him as heir to "the terrible Caraffa," as they called Pope Paul IV, and as the Inquisition incarnate. But he assured them: "I will act in such a way that Rome will regret my death more than my accession."

He was as good as his word. He was firm, severe, and implacable as he tried methodically to implement the disciplinary decrees of Trent. Bishops were ordered back to their dioceses under pain of imprisonment in the Castel San Angelo; the priests of Rome were reproved for allowing their congregations to laugh and joke in church and were informed such conduct must cease. No more galas and scandalous feasts or splendid processions of lordly cardinals! "He is no laughing matter," wrote the Venetian ambassador. Pius V could not suppress the Roman carnival, but he instituted the Forty Hours adoration as reparation for the licentiousness of the carnival, and during those days he spent his time in penitential exercises.

He pressed forward on all fronts, secular and political no less than religious, and while perhaps the secular historian remembers him best for his calling the last Crusade, which culminated in the Battle of Lepanto, his most significant accomplishment in the six years of his pontificate was surely the editing and publication of those four books which the Council of Trent held to be fundamental and indispensable. These were the Catechism of the Council of Trent, published in 1566; the reformed Breviary, published in 1568; the new Roman Missal, published in 1570; and the *Summa* of St. Thomas, which he commissioned in 1567, the same year in which he proclaimed St. Thomas a doctor of the Church. In a word, he set an example of fidelity to the teaching and decrees of the Council of Trent, an example that could not be ignored by anyone claiming the name of Catholic.

A few words are in order on the reformed Breviary and Missal. The Breviary had become very bulky and unwieldy due to many additions over the centuries; moreover, in the time of Pope Leo X (c. 1515) someone got the idea of introducing into the Breviary mythological "hymns" and other pretty things dear to the humanists—shades of our own times and *their* desecration of the liturgy! A Breviary in which our Lady was described as "blessed goddess" and the Trinity as "three-fold visage of Olympus" was surely in need of reform.

The new Breviary was prepared by a commission of cardinals, who forthwith proceeded to work also on the new Missal. The latter eliminated the differences between the four rites hitherto used in the Western Church for celebration of Mass. These were the Roman, Milanese or Ambrosian, Gallican, and Mozarabic rites, which henceforth had to conform to the new order of the Mass. This they did, except for some small details which a few churches, such as Lyons and Milan, and a few orders, such as the Carthusians and Dominicans, retained.

The immense and fruitful labors of Pope St. Pius V and his collaborators were of course but a beginning, though most essential and indispensable. It was fifty years or more before all the decrees of Trent took full hold in the Church: from the very promulgation of the decrees there were not wanting those who sought to water them down. Indeed, the earliest commentators on the doctrinal decrees were what would today be called "liberals" or "progressives," a phenomenon we have all become aware of since the issuance of the documents of Vatican II.

The latter council, at first sight, stands in striking contrast to the Council of Trent, for there seemed no impelling need, no overwhelming desire for it. Had not the Church survived the French Revolution and its aftermath in Europe in a most astonishing fashion; and fortified by the definitions of the First Vatican Council in *Dei Filius* and *Pastor Aeternus*, had it not emerged stronger than ever after two world wars? Had it not been blessed with a succession of great popes, and, secure in doctrine and discipline, was it not about to continue its unprecedented expansion, aided by the rapidly developing facilitation of travel and global communications springing from the technological revolution? What, then, impelled Pope John XXIII, that interim or lame-duck successor to Pius XII, as he was occasionally and patronizingly called, to convoke a general council?

For one thing, there was unfinished business at Vatican I which had to be abandoned at the outbreak of the Franco-Prussian War and the occupation of Rome by Italian troops. Vatical I had, as we saw, finally laid to rest the ghost of the decree *Sacrosancta* of the Council of Constance by defining the doctrine of the primacy and infallibility of the pope. But because it had to be suspended, it had not paid any attention (or insufficient attention) to the role of the other successors of the apostles, the bishops, in the governance of the Church and in their relation to the head of the episcopal college, Peter's successor.

But this was not the only or overriding consideration in the mind of Pope John when he decided to convoke the council. As he said himself, he did not see any need for new definitions; he had in mind a pastoral council, one which would renew the Church and bring it up to date.

What on earth did he mean by renewal, updating—*aggiornamento*, as he called it—and where was the need for it? I have no doubt that Pope John subscribed to the age-old thesis *Ecclesia semper reformanda*. But why *now*, in the middle of the twentieth century, when the Church seemed secure, in doctrine and worship and in ecclesiastical discipline? Precisely because it *was* the middle of the twentieth century and humanity had entered a new era, seemingly a post-Christian one, in which the spread and triumph of materialism and atheism on a worldwide basis seemed assured, underpinned by the resounding successes of the scientific and technological revolution.

But was the Church not ready and as well prepared as ever she had been to face the hazards of a new era and new challenge? Alas, no! What has happened in the Catholic Church since the Second Vatican Council should have disabused us of that notion. Has it not become evident, and crystal clear, that the virus of Modernism and Neo-modernism, which Pope St. Pius X strove so valiantly to isolate and destroy, had deeply infected the Church and burst into full bloom during and after the council? In the providence of God, the upheaval and turmoil that has followed the council has been necessary to purge the Church and purify her of dross, to prepare her and us, her members, for what still lies ahead, for our testing in the crucible. If nothing else had come out of Vatican II but the magnificent dogmatic constitution on the Church, *Lumen Gentium,* we should be eternally grateful, for in that document we have the most complete vision of the Church that has been so far vouchsafed to mankind, a complete and integral vision of the entire people of God: pope, bishops, priests and religious, and laity, with Mary, the Mother of Christ, our head and our God—Mary, the Mother of the Church—occupying her rightful place.

It is a vision of the Church that will serve us well in our time of testing, a vision that in God's good time will lead to the restoration of unity among all who believe in the divinity of Christ and bear his name, a vision that modern man will also have to see, unless he wishes to destroy himself.

All the other documents of the Second Vatican Council logically flow from this fundamental constitution on the Church. As we study them, we see that the contrast with Trent and with the other great councils of the Church almost vanishes, for they are restatements of doctrines already defined or universally taught, or legitimate developments of doctrine. Their continuity with the unbroken tradition of Catholic teaching is attested to by the numerous quotations from and references to Scripture, the fathers and doctors of the Church, the great councils, and papal encyclicals and decrees. There is no doubt, also, that the characteristic note throughout is irenic, ecumenical, and pastoral, as desired by Pope John—no anathemas, no condemnations except by implication.

This is the council, then, whose teachings Pope Paul VI has constantly in mind, as he has repeatedly told us. On his election in June 1963 he indicated that the main program of his pontificate would be the completion and implementation of the council.

He intervened decisively in the council itself when he saw it was necessary, and two very important examples of his intervention come to mind. One is the explanatory and prefatory note he ordered published as an authentic norm of interpretation with every edition of the dogmatic constitution on the Church, *Lumen Gentium.* The note is a model of clarity and precise and very blunt expression. For example, it states that the term "college" is not to be understood as referring to a group of equals who entrust their power to their president, and then spells out what collegiality and collegial action really mean, namely, *one* manner in which the pope may rule the Church, the other being his *personal* rule. The second example is the careful formula he added to the final text of the dogmatic constitution on divine revelation, *Dei Verbum.* "It is not from Sacred Scripture alone that the Church draws her certainty about what has been revealed" (*D.V.*, 2:9).

On December 8, 1965, the papal brief declaring the Second Vatican Council closed was read. In it Pope Paul stated:

> All the constitutions, decrees, declarations and votes have been approved by the deliberation of the Synod, and promulgated by us . . . We decide moreover that all that has been established synodically is to be religiously observed by all the Faithful, for the glory of God and the dignity of the Church and for the tranquillity and peace of all men. We have approved and established these things . . . so that, as it be judged and described, all efforts

> contrary to these things, by whoever or whatever author-
> ity, knowingly or in ignorance, be invalid and worthless
> from now on.

I have quoted this brief because in it we find Pope Paul's official and explicit statement that the mind of the Second Vatican Council was his mind and that he intended to implement all the recommendations of the council. He had already begun to do so, for on September 15, 1965, with the *motu proprio "Apostolica Sollicitudo,"* he had established a permanent Synod of Bishops: "a body for the universal Church directly and immediately subject to our authority." He had become convinced of the necessity and importance of such a body during the council, he said.

In his homily during the Mass on October 11, 1969, with which the first meeting of this permanent synod began, Pope Paul alluded to its origin in the council's deliberations on the dogmatic constitution of the Church, saying: "We were the first to deduce a pleasing duty from this re-evocation of the Divine design concerning the Apostolic Office." He affirmed: "We believe we have already given proof of this will to give practical increase to episcopal collegiality, both by instituting the Synod of Bishops and in recognizing the Episcopal Conferences." He drew attention to the absolute necessity for the two principles of charity and unity as the basis of the criteria for the postconciliar progress of ecclesial communion at the level of episcopal collegiality.

The first criterion, which is an application of the principle of subsidiarity, must, however, be tempered with wise and humble prudence "so that the common good of the Church may not be compromised by multifarious and excessive particular autonomies which would be harmful to that unity and charity which must make the Church 'one heart and soul.'" The second criterion, pluralism, must be "defined in such a way that it does not interfere with the faith, which cannot allow it, nor with the general discipline of the Church, which does not permit arbitrary judgment and confusion."

It is evident from the above that Pope Paul VI did not intend to be a Paul IV and institute reform all on his own. It is equally evident, from what followed, that he did not intend to be a tool of the synod or just another member, even *primus inter pares.* "Let it be clear," he said,

> that the government of the Church must not take on the appearances or the norms of temporal regimes, which are today guided by democratic institutions that are sometimes irresponsible and going to excess, or by totalitarian forms that are contrary to the dignity of the man who is subject to them; *the government of the Church has an original form of its own, which aims to reflect in its expressions the wisdom and the will of its Divine Founder.* And it is in this respect that we must remember our supreme responsibility, which Christ wished to entrust to us when He gave Peter the keys of the Kingdom . . . a responsibility that tradition and the Councils attribute to our specific ministry as Vicar of Christ, Head of the Apostolic College, Universal Pastor and Servant of the Servants of God, and which *cannot be conditional on the authority, supreme though it be, of the Episcopal College,* which we are the first to wish to honor, defend and promote, *but which would not be such, were it to lack our support.*

A clear and ringing reaffirmation of Chalcedon and Vatican II, is it not?

Addressing the council of the general secretariat of the Synod of Bishops a few months later (May 15, 1970), the pope returned to the twin themes: his fidelity to the teachings of the council and his personal and unique role as interpreter and executor of these teachings. He expressed his satisfaction with the work of the synod so far, and went on to say:

> The dynamic effect of the recent Ecumenical Council is thus being developed for the greater good of the Church. As far as we are concerned, it is our firm intention to hold fast to its perspectives and to put them into practice untiringly, day after day, in our pastoral activity and service for the whole Church, nor shall we permit ourself to be influenced by certain unwanted pressures, perhaps motivated by lack of knowledge. In close union with you, . . . *we wish progressively to further the Council teaching in the life of the Church. . . . For our part, the Council stands, in fact, as the program of our pontificate.* It has been most consoling for us to learn lately that a member of your Council, Cardinal Francis Marty, Archbishop of Paris . . . has spoken of our "conciliar constancy."

The pope contrasted this opinion of Cardinal Marty with

those to the contrary, expressed by others, which had caused him amazement and sorrow. "These voices," he said,

> which wish to pass for that of the Council, disturb conciliar agreement, dissent from collegial harmony and are merely spokesmen for a certain theological opinion. *A particular theology, we take the opportunity of repeating, is not the Council,* even though it may be a legitimate opinion. *The Pope is not, and cannot be, either the supporter or the spokeman, still less the prisoner of any given school. He is the successor of St. Peter by will of Jesus Christ.* To him it falls as a primary duty to stand at the head of his brothers, and in close union with them to be a witness to the Faith of the Church of which he is the appointed spokesman, *authorized to expound the conciliar teaching in accord with its whole tradition. This is our mission: this, with the help of the Holy Spirit, is our service to the Church.*

It was, then, as supreme pastor, as authentic interpreter of the teachings of the council which he did so much to shape, and which he made his own by ratifying and promulgating the council documents, that Pope Paul undertook, over the years that have passed since then, the immense labor of implementing the recommendations of the council. Many of these, though vitally important to the renewal of the Church, desired by Pope John, and blueprinted by the council, are little known to the average Catholic. Some, such as the revision of the canon law, are still in process. But perhaps the best known, and which perhaps has created most controversy and even anguish among the faithful, is the reform of the liturgy and the calendar.

In announcing the reformed calendar (among other changes) in an address at the close of the consistory on April 28, 1969, the pope indicated that the liturgical year had undergone no radical change. What the reform sought to accomplish was twofold: first, to ensure "that the essential elements of each liturgical season emphasized more clearly the central importance of the Paschal Mystery of Christ" and, second, to use the birth date for the celebration of each saint as far as possible and to include in the universal calendar those whose historical and representative importance is greatest for the universal Church, leaving the others who are less well known to local veneration.

Now obviously the latter rearrangement was likely to give rise to the most dispute, for it involves matters of judgment. Everyone has his or her favorite saint who seemed to be downgraded by not being included as even an alternate in the universal calendar. But this obviously is a judgment that properly belongs to the Holy See and always has; a glance at the old Roman calendar should be sufficient to demonstrate that fact. And anyone who is interested in hagiography knows that many wonderful saints never "made it" to the universal Roman calendar, just as there are even more who have never been beatified, much less canonized.

In speaking about the new rite of the Mass to his general audience on November 19, 1969, after the new rite had been officially promulgated, Pope Paul made three very important statements in answer to three questions posed by himself:

1. How could such a change be made? "It is due to the will expressed by the Ecumenical Council held not long ago." He then repeated verbatim the pertinent and specific recommendations of the constitution on the liturgy (*S.C.n.* 50), and added: "The reform . . . is therefore a response to an authoritative mandate from the Church. *It is an act of obedience* . . . it is not an arbitrary act. It is not a transitory or optional experiment. It is not some dilettante's improvisation. *It is a law.*"

2. What exactly are the changes? "You will see for yourselves that they consist of many new directions for celebrating the rites—simplification of the Entrance, Offertory and Communion rites, reinstitution of some ancient canons, as well as some simplifications of the Roman Canon," etc. "But keep this clearly in mind," he added, *"nothing has been changed of the substance of our traditional Mass. . . .* The Mass of the New Rite is and remains the same Mass we have always had."

The pope adverted to the possibility that some people might think that changes in the rite or the rubrics concealed some alteration or diminution of truths which are acquired by the Catholic faith forever and compromised the equation between the law of prayer, *lex orandi*, and the law of faith, *lex credendi*. "It is not so, absolutely not!" he exclaimed. "*Above all, because the Rite and the relative rubric are not in themselves a dogmatic definition.*"

3. What will be the results of this innovation? "The results expected, or rather desired, are that the Faithful will participate in the Liturgical Mystery with more understanding, in a more practical, a more enjoyable and a more sanctifying way. That is, they will hear the Word of God . . . and share in the mystical reality of Christ's sacramental and propitiatory Sacrifice."

Thank God such results are already evident, in many places and among many people—horror stories about maverick priests and aberrant liturgies notwithstanding. We must remember that such deviations were not authorized either by the council or by the Holy See. But what can be said about Pope Paul's right to make such changes, and what about *Quo Primum*? From Pope Paul's words, quoted above, two answers are immediately apparent:

1. His right to make such changes is witnessed by a correlative self-imposed duty: the duty of implementing the recommendations of the Second Vatican Council. This is not to say that he was the prisoner of the council, so to speak, or that the council could bid him obey. That would be to resurrect the decree *Sacrosancta* of the Council of Constance. Pope Paul accepted, ratified, and promulgated *all* the documents of Vatican II, and by so doing constituted them an exercise of the most solemn magisterium of the Church—a general council with the pope at its head.

2. A rite and the related rubrics are not in themselves a dogmatic definition; therefore the rite of the Mass or any of the sacraments may be changed by the reigning pope, *motu proprio*, as is said. We should recall that the Tridentine rite was imposed on the Western Church, with very minor alterations allowed, and it superseded four other rites in common use prior to Trent. But we hear good and faithful Catholics say: Did not Pope St. Pius V in *Quo Primum*

impose the Tridentine rite on the Western Church for all time? The answer is *he did not, because he could not,* because of the way it was done. No pope can bind his successors save only by a definition *de fide,* either *ex cathedra* or with a general council.

The formula in *Quo Primum* can be seen to be a common ending in most (if not all) papal bulls or decrees. Did we not read something similar in Pope Paul's brief with which the Second Vatican Council was terminated: "So that . . . all efforts contrary to these things . . . be invalid and worthless *from now on*"?

Let us make our own the affirmation of Erasmus, the great sixteenth-century humanist, when he broke with Luther: "I rely for certitude on nothing but the sure judgment of the Church." We have only one pope, one vicar of Christ, the current reigning pontiff. Let us heed him when he urges us, "Hold fast to the Council . . . we have a lamp to light our road" (address of January 14, 1970). Only thus can we hope, as St. Jerome Emilian hoped, "to re-establish Christendom in the most perfect state of sanctity."

3. Papal Primacy and Infallibility: What Does Pope Paul Have to Say?

The introductory pages of this book were devoted to a historical review of the development of the Church's thinking and teaching on these vitally important topics which culminated in the definitive documents of the First and Second Vatican Councils. We saw that the doctrine of the primacy of the pope as ruler and teacher was held from the very beginning and was reaffirmed on many occasions by individual popes and councils. We also recognized that one of the great unsettling events in the history of this belief was brought about by one of the general councils of the Church, the Council of Constance in 1414, which, in its decree *Sacrosancta*, declared in effect that all members of the Church, including the pope, are subject to the jurisdiction of a lawful general council. It was pointed out, however, that *Sacrosancta* was not ratified by the legitimate pope, who had been elected by that very council. The decree, therefore, was not binding on the Church. Nevertheless, its influence and effects were felt in the Church for centuries, and although it seemed that the ghost of *Sacrosancta* should have been finally laid to rest by the Vatican I definitions in *Pastor Aeternus*, it is legitimate to wonder if the ghost may have been revived and revitalized since Vatican II.

It is common knowledge that the authority of the Holy
See has come under increasing attack in the past decade or
more. On the one hand, we find the Neo-modernists—the
proponents of historical relativism, doctrinal relativism, and
process theology—disputing papal authority, juridical as
well as doctrinal. But we also see, regretfully, many of
those who call themselves traditional Catholics seemingly
aligned with these dissenters, at least *de facto*. These traditional Catholics of course maintain their belief, *explicitly*, in
the defined doctrines of the papal primacy and infallibility,
but they come perilously close to an *implicit* denial when
they criticize Pope Paul because he does not exercise the
power of the keys *as they think he should*. In essence, they
wish to substitute their judgment for his.

We have discussed this aspect of the problem on a previous occasion; so I will merely reiterate that it is incom-
patible with a full understanding and acceptance of the doctrine of the primacy and infallibility of the pope. That
doctrine, as defined in *Pastor Aeternus*, laid down the following:

1. Christ appointed Peter the first of all the apostles and
   the visible head of the whole Church by appointing him
   immediately and personally to the primacy of jurisdiction.
2. Peter was to have successors in the primacy for all
   time.
3. The successors of Peter in the primacy are the bishops
   of Rome.
4. The pope possessses full and supreme power of jurisdiction over the whole Church, not merely in matters of
   faith and morals but also in Church disciplines and in
   the government of the Church.
5. The Roman pontiff is personally infallible when he
   speaks *ex cathedra*, and his definitions are irreformable
   of themselves and not in virtue of the consent of the
   Church.

To which may be added the following words from *Lumen
Gentium*, the dogmatic constitution on the Church, promul-

gated at the Second Vatican Council:

> All this teaching about the institution, the perpetuity, the force and reason for the Sacred Primacy of the Roman Pontiff and of his infallible teaching authority, this Sacred Synod again proposes to be firmly believed by all the faithful. . . . For in virtue of his office, that is as Vicar of Christ and Pastor of the whole Church, the Roman Pontiff has *full, supreme, and universal power over the Church. And he can always exercise this power freely.* [*L.G.,* 3:18, 22]

It is also necessary to remind ourselves that this and all other documents of Vatican II were ratified and promulgated by the pope, as was essential if they were to have any binding force.

So, in a very real sense, we already have the answer to our question, what does Pope Paul say about papal primacy and infallibility? The answer is spelled out very clearly, but let me say it once more: *Lumen Gentium* sets forth authoritatively the mind of the Church and the mind of Pope Paul on this question, or he would not have ratified and promulgated it.

But, the objection is raised, by his actions and words since the council Pope Paul has apparently downgraded and diluted the authority of the Holy See, delegating it to the Synod of Bishops and to national episcopal conferences. And in the name of pluralism and freedom of conscience he has allowed heresy and heretics to flourish in the Church and play havoc with the faith; thus he is not exercising the power of the keys. There are some who go so far as to allege that the real Pope Paul is dead, that an imposter has taken his place, and that this has been confirmed by private revelations, attributed to the Mother of God!

Let us hear some of the pertinent statements of this "imposter." In an audience address of April 3, 1968, Pope Paul VI asked:

> Have you understood the significance of the symbolic name of Peter given by Jesus to His chief disciple . . . ? The concept Jesus wanted to express is clear . . . it is the concept of the solidity, stability, permanence . . . immovableness . . . the gift and the charism of strength, toughness, a rock-like power to resist and sustain; He

linked His message to the new and wonderful virtue of this Apostle who, *together with his lawful successors,* was to bear witness with incomparable security to that same message which we call the Gospel. Think it over carefully. Here we are over the tomb of Simon, renamed Peter. We recall and test the truth of the words of Jesus: here that Rock . . . is still firm, solid and secure. It is a historical, psychological, theological and wonderful miracle.

Many wish to submit truth to a radical revision . . . by changing the formulas in which the Teaching Church has expressed and, as it were, sealed it, to enable it to traverse the centuries while jealously preserving its identity. Then they alter the very content of traditional doctrine . . . the word of Christ . . . becomes a partial truth . . . deprived of all objective validity and transcendent authority. It will be said that the Council authorized such treatment of traditional teaching. *Nothing is more false. . . .* Faithfulness to the Council demands a fresh and wise study of the truth of the Faith and leads us back to the perennial, univocal and consoling testimony of St. Peter. *Jesus wanted His infallible voice to guarantee the stability of the Faith.*

But that was in 1968, supporters of the imposter theory will say; it was after the issuance of *Humanae Vitae* that the real Pope Paul was replaced. This is evident, they say, since only a bogus pope could have ignored *Quo Primum* and replaced the Mass of St. Pius V with a "heretical" version in 1969. They ignore the evident facts that the essential parts of the Mass are unchanged, that the Tridentine rite was once an innovation and displaced other ancient and legitimate rites, and that, as Pope Paul said, a rite is not a doctrinal definition and therefore is reformable.

But anything said by the pope since 1969 carries no weight with such people, even when he patiently and repeatedly restates defined doctrine. On April 26, 1969, he said to his audience visitors:

You have come to see Peter . . . to have the vision of and the tangible experience of the Pope . . . because he is *Simon petrified* . . . to touch the Rock . . . to assure yourselves that it is not worn away by the centuries, nor by the whirling storms of history. . . . In fact this is living rock . . . from which there gushes forth a spring that is always capable of quenching the thirst of the human community that gathers around it and forms the edifice of the Church . . . the Mystical Body of Christ.

Empty rhetoric, they will say, cleverly crafted in the style of the real Pope Paul and delivered by a consummate impersonator and mimic who has had plastic surgery. And who but a bogus pope would pay what he called "a fraternal Christian visit" to Geneva on June 10, 1969, and ask, "Is not the World Council of Churches a marvelous movement of Christians, of 'Children of God who are scattered abroad,' who are now searching for a recomposition of unity?"

But let us hear what else he said. "We are here among you," he stated. *"Our name is Peter. Scripture tells us which meaning Christ has willed to attribute to this name, what duties He lays upon Us—the responsibilities of the Apostle and his Successors. But permit us to recall other titles which the Lord wished to give to Peter to signify other charisms. Peter is Fisher of Men; Peter is Shepherd."*

Having spoken of the Christian fellowship which exists between all the baptized, the work of the secretariat for promoting Christian unity, theological dialogue, ecumenical collaboration, and the norms established for this collaboration by the Second Vatican Council's decree on ecumenism, the pope asked boldly: "In view of all this, should the Catholic Church become a member of the World Council?" And he answered: "In fraternal frankness we do not consider that the question is so mature that a positive answer could or should be given. The question still remains a hypothesis." These are surely not the words of an imposter, and there is no evidence that any members of the World Council of Churches, gathered in Geneva that day, had any doubt they were seeing and hearing the real Pope Paul VI.

Only one conclusion is reasonable in connection with this story of a bogus pope. It is the work of the Father of Lies, an attempt to lead the simple pious faithful astray, to alienate them from their Catholic loyalty to a *living* magisterium, from the *living* vicar of Christ on earth.

Listen to him less than three weeks after his visit to Geneva, on the Feast of St. Peter, his predecessor. He invited his audience to "begin with a meditation on something of capital importance in the design of our Faith," namely, what Sacred Scripture relates about Simon, his mission and position as chief of the apostles, and the function immediately exercised by him in the nascent Christian community. "That function," Pope Paul stated, "was one of being Center, Teacher and Head," confirmed by the facts of his ministry, the historical development of his mission in the Church, and the theological reflections on it down to the last two ecumenical councils. These reflections, he said, should inspire the feelings and sentiments "proper to those who have gathered to honor that Apostle who more than any other assures us of our communion with Christ, who inspires us with simple, filial and devout confidence, precisely because of those Blessed Keys, the Keys no less than of the Kingdom of Heaven, which the Lord placed in his hands."

And to what further insights should these reflections and sentiments lead, asked the Holy Father:

> Peter is here, what shall we ask him? We have to ask Peter for the Faith, that which comes to us from him and from the Apostles, that which we openly professed on this same feast last year, the Faith of the entire Church. . . . We are also required to have fidelity, loyalty. . . . We ask this of Peter as the man who, as head of the Apostles and of all who would be associated with him in the Faith, had from Christ the incomparable favor of a prayer, uttered by Christ Himself, so that he should be strong in Faith. *He also received the infallible mandate to confirm his brethren* after his hour of weakness. . . . *He had the primacy of love for Christ and therefore had pastoral primacy toward his flock.*

Let us step forward three years to the eve of that same Feast of St. Peter in 1972, when Pope Paul recalled once more for his audience some of the salient facts about St. Peter: first, his name, given him by the Lord himself in the very proclamation of his plan to build his Church on the foundation stone of this man, Simon; then the symbol of the keys, the gift of which is the investiture with power over the whole house. "What house? The Kingdom of Heaven, the economy of salvation, the mysterious plan of supernatural order . . . installed by Christ between God and man. *Peter, and with him the college of the other Apostles, is nominated as the intermediary necessary for normal access to the Kingdom of Heaven.*"

There is the symbol of the net, signifying the nature of the evangelical and apostolic mission; the boat, from which the Lord often taught the people, a timely and appropriate symbol of the Church as haven, as ark, "sailing on the waves of time and history, which still appears as the coat of arms of Peter in the seal used to this day to give authenticity to the most important documents of the Church, the Fisherman's Ring." Pope Paul did not gloss over the sign of the cock, the extraordinary and dramatic story of Peter's triple denial, foretold by our Lord, and surely intended to underline the absolute necessity of divine grace and the divine guarantee in making Peter and his successors the foundation of the Church. This reflection leads naturally to the symbolism of the shepherd, the pastor.

"Just think," Pope Paul exclaimed, "Peter the Pastor, living in his successors; the perpetual and visible source and foundation of unity—in Faith, Hope and Charity! He who is speaking to you now, exults and trembles when evoking these evangelical images concerning Peter, in whom the Church honors Jesus Christ today; and you can understand why."

We surely can, unless we stop our ears and blind our eyes and close our minds and hearts.

"So say a prayer also for us," Pope Paul concluded, "the unworthy but true successor of Peter."

It is clear from reading many of Pope Paul's addresses, not to mention the more formal documents ratified and promulgated by him, such as *Mysterium Ecclesiae*, that he knows who he is: the vicar of Christ on earth, the successor of St. Peter in the primacy as bishop of Rome—"the perpetual and visible source and foundation of unity." He has no identity crisis!

But what are we to say to those who allege that Pope Paul has, in practice, abdicated his responsibility and authority in favor of the College of Bishops and national episcopal conferences? He has indeed emphasized and, as he said, carried out the self-imposed "duty of giving wider and more operative efficacy to the collegial character of the Episcopate," a duty he deduced from the documents of the Second Vatican Council on the Church and the role of bishops in her governance. We cannot in a short space deal exhaustively with this topic; so let us hear what the pope had to say on the matter in a few addresses.

He spoke of it on October 11, 1969, when he concelebrated Mass with the participants in the extraordinary Synod of Bishops, and again at its conclusion on October 27, 1969. At the outset he recalled that the concept of collegiality was not new but was simply taken up anew at the council; it was a re-evocation of the divine design concerning the apostolic office. He recalled what he had already done to implement the council's recommendations for this renewed emphasis on the principle and practice of collegiality. He also made important statements on the nature of collegiality, and his characterization can be summed up in three simple propositions:

1. Collegiality is charity—a charity fuller and more binding even than the bond of charity, uniting *all* the faithful.
2. Collegiality is coresponsibility—a common sensitiveness for the general and particular needs of the Church.
3. Collegiality is unity—the perpetual and *visible* source and foundation of this unity is the lawful successor of St. Peter, the Roman pontiff.

These principles must be applied in developing guidelines for collegiality in practice so that recognition is given "in fairer measure to that fullness of prerogative and power that comes to our brothers in the Episcopate *in virtue of the sacramental character of their election* to pastoral functions in the Church, *and which derives from their effective communion with this Holy See.*"

Is it not clear that the pope was reminding the bishops that he acknowledges their prerogatives and power, but that these stem from their episcopal ordination, and the latter in turn from their relation with the Holy See? But as if to drive the point home, he reminded them of two other important and fundamental facts:

1. "The government of the Church has an original form of its own which aims to reflect in its expressions the wisdom and the will of its Divine Founder."

2. His own supreme responsibility, "which," he said, "Christ wished to entrust to us when he gave Peter the Keys of the Kingdom . . . a responsibility that tradition and the Councils attribute to our specific ministry as Vicar of Christ, Head of the Apostolic College, Universal Pastor and Servant of the Servants of God, *and which cannot be conditional on the authority, supreme though it be, of the Episcopal College*, which we are the first to wish to honor, defend and promote, *but which would not be such, were it to lack our support*."

At the conclusion of the synod he thanked the participants and told them he would give the greatest consideration to their desires and recommendations: "an examination, the conclusion of which it will be our duty to meditate before Christ, in the intimacy of our conscience and with a sense of our responsibility as Supreme Pastor of the Holy Church of God. *Only then can we express our judgment in their regard*, a judgment that will be promptly communicated to you."

He indicated his confidence in the synod which had arisen from the teaching and spirit of the recent council, and which was intended "not to produce power, rivalry or difficulties for ordered and effective government with the Church, but rather as a mutual inclination of Pope and Episcopate for greater communion and organic collaboration." The pope continued:

> For our part we intend to bring all this to realization . . . obviously we will do so without, however, at any time renouncing in our turn our specific duties and responsibilities, which are imposed on us both by the charism of the Primacy conferred by Christ Himself on Peter, whose most lowly, yet authentic successor we are, and by the obligation, rather than the right, of exercising that Primacy faithfully. The Pope must be the Church's heart, to make charity which comes from the heart and goes to the heart. He must be a cross-road for charity, receiving all

and loving all, because Christ left us Peter as "The Vicar
of His Love." [St. Ambrose, *Exp. in Luc.,* 1, 8, 175; Pl.
15:1942]

Despite these clear and forthright statements of his actions
and intentions with respect to the council's recommendations
on collegiality and national episcopal conferences, it is evident that the Holy Father came in for sharp criticism, pre-
sumably from some bishops. It amazed and hurt him, to the
extent that he referred to it on May 15, 1970, when he received in audience members of the council of the general
secretariat of the Synod of Bishops. While we must deplore
such attacks and sincerely regret the anguish they must have
caused this pope, who has already surely put in his purgatory, we nevertheless can take some comfort from them for
they give the lie to those who allege Pope Paul has abdicated
his power and authority. On this occasion, too, the pope
made a ringing reaffirmation of his primacy and teaching
authority:

> These voices [he said, referring to his critics], which wish
> to pass for that of the Council, disturb conciliar agree-
> ment, dissent from collegial harmony and are merely
> spokesmen for a certain theological opinion. A particular
> theology, we take the opportunity of repeating, is not the
> Council, even though it may be a legitimate opinion.
> The Pope is not, and cannot be, either the supporter or
> the spokesman, still less the prisoner of any given school.
> He is the successor of St. Peter by will of Jesus Christ.
> To him it falls as a primary duty to stand at the head
> of his brothers, and in close union with them to be a
> witness to the Faith of the Church of which he is the
> appointed spokesman, authorized to expound the conciliar
> teaching in accord with its whole tradition. This is our
> mission; this, with the help of the Holy Spirit, is our
> service to the Church.

"Authorized to expound the conciliar teaching in accord
with its whole tradition"—namely, the entire tradition of
the Catholic Church. Let us dwell on that statement, which
ought to evoke memories of all those similar extraordinary
claims by popes throughout history. Does it not echo the
letter of Pope St. Celestine I to the Council of Ephesus, the
tome of Pope St. Leo the Great at Chalcedon, the letter of
Pope Agatho to the Third General Council of Constantinople,

not to mention the definitions of Vatican I and their reaffirmation and amplification in Vatican II?

The key statement of *Lumen Gentium,* the dogmatic constitution on the Church, says that "all this teaching about the institution, the perpetuity, the force and reason for the sacred primacy of the Roman Pontiff and of his infallible teaching authority, this Sacred Synod again proposes to be firmly believed by all the faithful" (*L.G.,* 3:18). True, the council forcefully reemphasized the power and authority of bishops and the College of Bishops, but let us not forget that the council also stated unequivocally that "the College or body of Bishops has no authority unless it is simultaneously conceived of in terms of its Head, the Roman Pontiff."

You may recall from earlier pages that Pope Paul ordered a prefatory note on this very topic to be an integral part of the constitution *Lumen Gentium.* It was to serve as *the* authentic norm of interpretation for chapter 3, which treats the collegiality of bishops and their relation to the pope. Let us read again the essential core of the prefatory note:

> For necessarily and always the College carries with it the idea of its Head, who preserves intact in the College his role of Vicar of Christ and Shepherd of the Universal Church. . . . The care of the whole flock of Christ has been entrusted to the Supreme Pontiff. It belongs to him . . . to determine the way in which it is fitting for this care to be exercised, whether personally or collegially. The Roman Pontiff proceeds according to his own discretion and in view of the welfare of the Church in structuring, promoting and endorsing any exercise of collegiality.
>
> As Supreme Pastor he can always exercise his authority as he chooses, as is demanded by the office itself. While the College always exists it is not always "in full act," indeed it operates through collegial actions only at intervals and only with the consent of its Head. The word *only* takes in every case . . . in every instance it is clear that the union of the bishops with their Head is contemplated, and never any action of the bishops taken independently of the Pope.

Clearly, there is a continuity of thought, belief, conviction, and even style between these words of Pope Paul in 1964, when *Lumen Gentium* was ratified and promulgated, and the pope whose addresses in the late sixties and early seventies we have just been quoting. Clearly it is the same mind, the same man.

Let us remember his statement, "as Supreme Pastor he can always exercise his authority as he chooses," when we hear criticism of his failure to exercise the power of the keys. Let us remember it, as we conclude this chapter, by trying to see this pope as he sees himself. On the eve of his journey to the Far East in November 1970, he spoke to a general audience and drew a graphic picture:

> The scene is history, our own history, our own time, today, in which we are looking for "the signs of the times." It is an uneven scene . . . full of light and darkness . . . devastated by the blasts of apparently irresistible hurricanes — modern ideologies; yet there are also a few spring breezes — the breath of the Spirit, who "blows where He will."
>
> There are three actors on this stage: one, filling it completely, is the incalculable number of the people of today, growing, rising, aware as never before. . . . They know about everything and are skeptical about everything and their own destiny. They are unbridled in the flesh and foolish in the mind. . . . One feature seems to be common to all of them: they are unhappy, something essential is lacking. Who can get near them? Who can instruct them about the things that are necessary for life, when they know so many superfluous things? Who can interpret them and, through truth, resolve the doubts that are tormenting them? Who can reveal to them the call which they have implicitly in their hearts? These crowds are an ocean — they are humanity. They hold the stage and are passing slowly but tumultuously across it. . . .
>
> But there enters another character. He is small, like an ant, weak, unarmed. . . . He tries to make his way through the throng; he is trying to say something. He becomes unyielding and tries to make himself heard; he assumes the appearance of a teacher, a prophet . . . you will have guessed who he is — the Apostle, the messenger of the Gospel. . . . In this case it is the Pope, daring to pit himself against mankind. David and Goliath? Others will say Don Quixote. . . . But when he manages to obtain a little silence and attract a listener, the little man speaks in a tone of certainty which is all his own. He utters inconceivable things, mysteries of an invisible world which is yet near us, the Divine world, the Christian world, but mysteries. Some laugh, others say to him — we will hear you another time. . . . However someone has listened and always listens, and

has perceived two singular accents — the accent of truth and the accent of love. They perceive that the word is the speaker's only in the sense that he is an instrument: it is a Word in its own right, the Word of Another. Where was that Other, and where is He now? He could not and cannot be other than a living being, a Person who is essentially a Word, a Word made man, the Word of God. Where was and where is the Word of God made man? For it was and is now clear that He was and is now present! And this is the third actor on the world stage who stands above it all and fills the whole stage wherever He is welcomed. O Christ, it is You."

Yes, Pope Paul clearly sees himself as the legitimate successor of St. Peter, as apostle and evangelizer, as bishop of Rome and of the universal Church, as supreme pontiff and head of the College of Bishops, with whom that college must be in harmony if it is to have the mind of Christ, "authorized," as he said, "to expound the conciliar teaching in accord with its *whole* tradition," because he recognizes that he *is* the vicar of Christ on earth—the sign and foundation of that unity of the entire Church for which the Lord prayed so earnestly and repeatedly at the Last Supper.

Yes, but like the Master a sign of contradiction! No wonder, in this age of widespread apostasy and rebellion against his lawful authority and magisterial teaching, that his posture is like that of John the Baptist—"He [Christ] must increase and I must decrease." Can we, his loyal sons and daughters, criticize him if he imitates the Christ of the Parable of the Weeds rather than the Christ who made a whip of cords and drove the moneychangers and other hucksters from the temple?

Pope Paul, year in and year out, has spoken out and condemned all deviations from the revealed truth of Christ. He has implied that many who follow these deviations are self-excommunicated, *ipso facto*, as is said, though they refuse to acknowledge the fact. If he chooses not to name names and pronounce formal edicts of excommunication, that is his decision to make, and his alone. To believe and say otherwise would be to join the self-excommunicated in their misery and foolish pride.

4. What Has Pope Paul Been Doing?

This question is not intended to be frivolous or impertinent. Rather it is meant to focus attention on a very fundamental necessity, namely, getting to know "the manifest mind and will" of the Holy Father as expressed in his own words, especially at his weekly general audiences and other public events.

Another question is neither rhetorical nor unnecessary: Why should we be interested in what Pope Paul has been doing? The answer is essentially simple yet profound. Because he is pope, the vicar of Christ on earth!

What does this mean? Do we realize fully what this implies? We shall see what it means to Pope Paul himself. But what does it mean to us when we say we believe that the reigning pope is the vicar of Christ? What *should* it mean?

Recall our divine Lord's response to his disciples when they asked him to tell them the sign of his coming and of the end of the world. As St. Matthew tells it: "In answer Jesus said to them, 'Take care that no one leads you astray. For many will come in My name saying, 'I am the Christ.' . . . Then if anyone say to you 'Behold, here is the Christ,' or 'There He is,' *do not believe it.*" (Matt. 24:4–6, 23, 24)

Recall also that St. John, in his first epistle, wrote of the power of Antichrist, of whom he said, "Now you must know that he is here in the world already" (1 John 4:3).

How can we discern the false prophets of whom our Lord spoke? How discern the Antichrist of whom St. John wrote? There is no other way than by holding fast to Peter, by keeping our eyes and our ears fixed on his successor in the primacy, the vicar of Christ; by believing with St. Ambrose, *"Ubi Petrus, ibi Ecclesia"*; by realizing that when the Holy Father speaks to us on matters of faith and morals we are listening to our divine Lord. This is what it means to be a Catholic.

What, then, has Pope Paul been doing? He has been doing many, many things, but he has been doing two things in superlative fashion: teaching and suffering.

Teaching: Petrus Docens

The rest of our study will consider Pope Paul's actions and teachings in many areas of Catholic doctrine and practice, but this section is concerned with the teachings of Pope Paul that bear on two topics: (1) belief in God and (2) defense of the Church and preaching love for her and loyalty.

Belief in God

It may seem strange and rather incomprehensible that nearly 2,000 years after that "fullness of time" spoken of in Scripture, when God sent his only-begotten Son, the pope should find it desirable, even necessary, to recall us to that most fundamental fact, accessible to human reason, the existence of God. But a little reflection should help dispel any puzzlement.

Belief in God has been so much a part of us that we find it hard to realize there are immense numbers of people, people we meet in everyday life as well as those we read about, for whom God is dead. We need to open our eyes and look around us for daily evidence of what the council fathers of Vatican II spoke about so succinctly and gravely, namely, the absence of the thought of God, of faith in God, in modern man (*G.S.*, 19, 20). Surely we cannot fail to realize it in this place and at this time, when God's most innocent creatures, the "unwanted" unborn, have been declared non-persons by virtue of the practical atheism of seven men in the Supreme Court of the United States; when, as a result, every day thousands of these little ones, whose angels see the face of God in heaven, are delivered by their mothers to the new barbarians. So we should have little difficulty agreeing that the fundamental problem we face in this twentieth century, the characteristic mark of our "brave new world," is *practical atheism.*

Pope Paul, in an address on November 13, 1968, must have startled his audience by asking, "Do you know where you are?" Unlike so many of our modern sophists, he proceeded to give an answer:

> Here God is known. Here God is loved. Here God is present. Because here is the heart of the Church; here is Christ in His operating salvific power. . . . Here God is at home. . . . Here everything speaks of that God who outside, in the secular world, is said to be dead. No contradiction is more violent and sacrilegious than the one exploding from these two terms, God and death, if they are considered in their objective meaning . . . but we know that this unhappy slogan is applied in cultural language to its subjective meaning, that is, to the thought of man. . . . *God is dead in the mind of man. It is not the sun that has ceased to shine; it is man's eye that is plunged in darkness.*

He went on to speak of religious indifference, secularization as a process of thought, the discarding of metaphysics, and the claim of atheism, in the name of science, to be a liberation, a conquest. "Knowledge of God is impossible, it is argued; moreover, it is useless, even harmful."

For the Church, he says, "God is not dead and [the Church] continues undaunted and happy, to testify and announce, with Peter, Christ the Son of the Living God, and to celebrate the glory of God with blessed certainty."

> There are some people who find this surviving voice strange, so that they predict that it will not last, or it will conform to the equivocal theologies of modern incredulity, of post-Christianity. . . . It is not this inauspicious prophecy that frightens us. . . . What concerns us is the increased difficulty of communicating our religious

> message to men. . . . *Man is less available for the religious idea and life today than he was yesterday.*

One would have to say, from daily experience, that this is almost an understatement.

Modern man, especially "educated" man, appears not only totally oblivious of the transcendent God and of any idea of religion, but complacent about this oblivion, a complacency that is ruffled only when one dares to suggest that there might be considerations other than "humanitarian," scientific, or professional principles relevant to a discussion, for instance, of bioethical problems. One is made aware that one has been guilty of an unpardonable and unwarranted intrusion! And this is not only in the neo-pagan milieu of the secular university. Many of our Catholic institutions of higher learning have become so secularized, so bewitched by the "signs of the times," so seduced by the mammon of state or federal support that, in effect, academic freedom has come to mean liberty to teach error only. The magisterial teachings of the Church or the legitimate authority of the ordinary of the diocese are regarded as an intolerable intrusion.

"Modern man," the pope says, "has, more than man in the past, the need and the ability to get in touch with the mystery of God, but he is not as ready as his ancestors to meet and admit this necessary and inevitable mystery." Why? "Because he has widened the scope of his study and observation and has immensely extended the field of his sensible experience; and he is therefore tempted to feel satisfied with what he knows scientifically and through the senses."

But this is not the only reason. The Holy Father pointed also to an elementary and fundamental truth: *God is hidden!* True, he has revealed himself to us by many signs, in many ways, by many voices; he has given us the light of rational thought, above all the light of faith, which is fuller, surer, more alive. Nevertheless, in this life we see him reflected in mystery, "through a glass darkly" (1 Cor. 13:12).

The pope returned to this theme again and again over the ensuing weeks. The very next week, on November 20, 1968, he began his address as follows: "Listen to these simple and amazing words: We must search for God! . . . Now we say, we must seek God! And the first reason is perfectly obvious: Because He is hidden!"

The following week, on November 27, 1968, again he cried out: "How can we know God? This is the great question tormenting the modern spirit. It is a question as old as the history of man."

" 'God is not an invention, He is a discovery,' " the Holy Father answers, quoting the French author Zundel (*Recherche du Dieu inconnu*, p. 7). He points out with St. Thomas that, while by reason we arrive at knowing what God is not, what he is in his intimate essence remains quite unknown to us; and though we must be happy with the immense and luminous knowledge of God provided us by faith and our religious doctrine, God must always be sought, God must always be discovered. "He must be sought endlessly because He must be loved endlessly. . . . The greater the love, the more must one seek to know what the search has revealed," said St. Augustine (*Enarr. in Ps.*, 104:3; Pl. 37: 1392).

The pope answers decisively the specious arguments of the secular humanists with the striking statement: "The so-called 'Death of God' ends in the death of man."

But, he insisted, "the question remains: How are we to advance along such inaccessible paths?"

The answer, the pope says, again quoting St. Thomas, is that *"it is sufficient to use reason well"* (II, II, 4, 5, 2). "Everyone can do this, even uneducated persons," he declared; "in fact simple souls, children, humble people, the pure of heart particularly, have a healthier and more convincing natural logic than those who in the development of their reason have violated, or forgotten, certain of its exigencies." The crisis of faith can be solved by purifying our ideas of God and his worship: we seek God in thought and find him in love.

The crisis can also be solved in another way, the pope tells us: "By logically pushing the materialistic world to its inevitable consequences, which finally appeal to God in order not to fall into monstrous and catastrophic conceptions of pseudo-absolute and inhuman forms of life."

"This painful and amazed cry," he prophesied, "will have to be raised to God one day by the modern world, which has mastered things and become deeply enslaved to them; and it will be a great day, a day of salvation and poetry, in which God will appear as He is for us, 'the source of existence, the norm of truth, the law of love' (St. Augustine, *Contra Faustum* 20:7; Pl. 42:372); the eternal new, the silent word, the invisible presence, the joyful treasure, the total principle, living being."

The Holy Father, however, did not confine himself to philosophizing about God. In his address of December 18, 1968, he returned to the doctrine which is tormenting modern man: the doctrine on God. But on this occasion he said: "We know a fundamental truth: We have a teacher! More than a teacher, an Emmanuel, that is, God with us; we have Jesus Christ!"

It is not that before the incarnation God was unknown; the fact remains, as stated by St. John in the first chapter of his gospel: "No man has ever seen God; but now His Only, Begotten Son, who abides in the bosom of the Father, has made Him known."

"It is obvious, therefore, that Christ sits as teacher in the Conciliar Chair" (*Dei Verbum*, N. 4).

The pope dealt succinctly with the modern non-Catholic evaluation of Christ as "a particularly good man," "the man for others." "He is measured," he said, "with a human yardstick and accepted for what He can serve today, a humanitarian and sociological purpose." And he referred to the accusation against the Church, so often heard nowadays, even among Catholics, "that She has shut Him up in dogmatic formulas that are incomprehensible and outdated."

> But we wish to warn you to remain strong in the Faith.
> We must adhere to the words of the Pontiff, St. Leo
> the Great, the theologian of the mystery of the Incarnation: "The word of God, God Himself because He is
> the Son of God . . . became Man: Stooping to assume
> our littleness, without renouncing His greatness, in such

> a way as to remain what He was and to assume what
> He was not, and to unite the true nature of the servant
> with the nature that He had, identical with that of God
> the Father" [*Serm. XXI;* Pl. 54:192].
>
> This is the Doctrine of Chalcedon; it is the Doctrine
> of the Catholic Church. . . . She does not change;
> She does not mutilate the truth, of which She is the
> depository; and it will always be possible for everyone
> to find once more the true face of Christ, and in Christ's
> face the vision, now possible for us, of the Father, as
> well as the vision of man, which is always to be discovered
> more and more.

These words of Pope Paul are a simple yet profound summary of his Christology and ecclesiology, as well as a recapitulation of the constant teaching of the supreme magisterium. Christ is the final revelation of the Father because he is the only-begotten Son, consubstantial with the Father in his divine nature—the final revelation by means of the incarnation; and the depository of the truth of God's revelation is the Church. Only in the Church can we find the true face of Christ, risen and ascended in glory, and in his face not only the vision of the Father but also the true vision of man.

Defense of the Church and Preaching Love for Her and Loyalty

The Holy Father developed and amplified his vision of the Church in many subsequent addresses, defending her and appealing for love and fidelity toward her—our second topic.

On May 7, 1969, he said to those attending his general audience:

> Our desire would be to confirm and increase in you love
> for the Church, for the Holy Church of Christ, which is,
> as you know, the Mystical Body of Christ, the extension
> of the mystery of the Incarnation in humanity and time.
> It is the sign and instrument of the economy of salvation
> on the one hand; the term and plenitude of the redeeming
> work of Christ Himself on the other hand. The Church is
> the means and the Church is the end with regard to the
> kingdom of Christ.

These are very plain words, unmistakable in their meaning. But, one may ask, was he referring to the ideal Church or to the real Church as it appears to us today? The pope made it clear that he spoke of the vision of the Church in its ideal and also real truth, despite its human imperfections: "It is a Holy, Sacred institution, but built with human material, always inadequate and frail"; hence always needing reform.

Such reform cannot be accomplished without much suffering—how much, we shall see later. The necessity for such suffering we can begin to see by reflection on Pope Paul's seminal statement that the Church is "the term and plenitude of the redeeming work of Christ Himself." Our divine Lord suffered because of our sins, and redeemed us by his sufferings and death on the cross. His mystical body, the Church, cannot but suffer if she is to carry forward the work of redemption until the end of time. And for the same reason: our sins, the sins of the members of his mystical body. "Not so!" cry the dissident Modernists; "it is the institutional Church that is at fault, the 'structures.' These must go! The people are the Church!"

Pope Paul reviewed this Modernist attack succinctly in this address and gave it a ringing answer:

> One word recurs continually in this polemical reformism: "the structures," which in the present phenomenon of illuministic contestation takes on the significance of canonical organism, juridical institutions, traditional ecclesiastic bodies, responsible hierarchical authorities, certain archaic systems, which form the skeleton of the ecclesial body, established dogmatic doctrines, authoritative magisterium, Roman Curia, etc. "The structures" correspond to the "institutional church," so called, in comparison with, and also in opposition to, the free and spiritual church. That is, they take on a negative meaning, and the new self-styled charismatic christianity, the christianity of free biblical interpretation, hurls injurious insinuations at it and claims arbitrary rights, both of judgment and of action. If religion is dying out, if the Church is deserted, it is the fault, they say, of "the structures," the obstacle lies in "the structures"; "the structures" are sclerosed, "the structures" do not derive from Christ; let us free ourselves of "the structures" and we will have a young authentic christianity once more.

Alas, in practice it turns out to be a "Christianity" without duties of any kind, only rights, rights of a conscience illumined only by perceived bodily and psychic needs, perceived as essential to self-fulfillment—a "Christianity" without Christ!

Of course, the pope realizes the need for reform of the "structures." It is already afoot, he tells us, while asking "who has the right to judge, who has the authority and the responsibility for deep innovating interventions?"

> We wish to give a warning to the supporters of sudden surgical simplifications. . . . The authentic youth of the Church will not be obtained by secularizing and liberalizing ecclesial life itself, that is by freeing it of its external structures . . . but rather by reviving within the Church the current of the life-bringing spirit, the life of prayer and grace, the exercise of charity, obedience and holiness. The voice of the prophet we heard during Lent still rings out: *"Rend your hearts, and not your clothes!"* (Joel 2:13)

Let us ask again the question posed by Pope Paul: "Who has the right to judge, who has the authority and the responsibility for deep innovating interventions?" We find he had answered it, implicitly, at an audience just ten days earlier, on April 26, 1969. He had opened his address with one of those seemingly artless questions that he frequently uses— "a discreet question," he called it. "Why did you come to this audience?" He put forward several tentative answers. To please the pope? Because here you are not strangers? Out of simple curiosity? To sample the atmosphere of a papal audience?

> We will tell you how you *should* answer. . . . You have come *"Videre Petrum,"* to see Peter — that is, to have the vision of, and, to a certain extent, the tangible experience of the Pope, not so much because he too is a person like all other men, but *because he is Simon petrified!*

In other words, because there is realized in him the marvelous charism of a solidity, a firmness, a stability charged with a divine promise and made evident, in a certain way, by historical survival. To have the vision, the tangible and personal experience of this phenomenon that is Peter. *Yes!* The Lord is still here, in his humble successor.

What is he doing? He is doing what Jesus decreed. "On

this rock I will build My Church" (Mt. 16:18). That is, he is acting as the base, the foundation, the support of that immense and troubled human family, which Christ defined as his Church.

Is this the ecclesiology of the dissident theologian, the schismatic bishop, the "liberal," "liberated" Catholic whose rule of faith is dictated by eclectic self-interest and intellectual pride? Let us hear further what the vicar of Christ says about the Church and his indispensable place and function in it.

> Here you come to touch the reality of this "sign and instrument" of the union re-established between men and God, and, moreover, of the unity of men among themselves, which is the Church, and to assure yourselves that the Rock, the stone, on which She is built, is not worn away by the centuries, nor by the whirling storms of history, but is always equally, miraculously firm. In fact . . . this is living rock, not motionless like a dead thing and deprived of spirit.
>
> It is a rock from which there gushes forth a spring that is always capable of quenching the thirst of the human community that gathers around it and forms the edifice of the Church . . . the Mystical Body of Christ.

Here is the true ecclesiology, here is the true vision of the Church, here is the Church to which the Holy Father constantly exhorts us to be loyal and faithful, which he repeatedly calls us to love, as on September 24, 1969, when he spoke of the Church's needs, which are also the needs of our souls. The needs he spoke of are a triple fidelity: fidelity to the religious and Christian manner of life of which we are the heirs; fidelity to authentic renewal founded on authorized and responsible evaluation—really, fidelity of obedience to the magisterium; and fidelity of love—love for the Bride of Christ "without spot or wrinkle or any such thing. . . . Holy and without blemish" (Eph. 5:27). "Fill your hearts," he cried, "with that love that was in the heart of Christ Himself; '*Dilexit Ecclesiam*, He loved the Church,' as St. Paul said" (Eph. 5:25).

There are many other addresses by Pope Paul which set out in simple yet profound words his teachings on the Church, of which he is the visible head, the cornerstone.

They are for the most part reiterations of what he wrote in his encyclical on the Church, *Ecclesiam Suam,* and of the dogmatic constitution on the Church, *Lumen Gentium,* of the Second Vatican Council, which he made his own and which has inspired so much of his teaching.

It should be clear from what we have reviewed that in the mind of Pope Paul there is a logical and inevitable progression, from belief in God to belief in his divine Son-made-man to belief in the Church which He founded on Peter and his successors in the primacy.

Suffering

The second superlative activity of the Holy Father, to which we alluded earlier, is suffering.

When we reflected on one of Pope Paul's key definitions of the Church as "the term and plenitude of the redeeming work of Christ Himself," we saw that this characterization of the Church implied suffering: *the Church is and must needs be a suffering Church.* The pope developed this theme in a wonderful manner in his general audience address of April 2, 1969, during Holy Week. He said:

> You find the Church not in festivity, but completely absorbed in a grave and sorrowful meditation on the passion of Christ, on His ineffable sufferings, on His Cross, on His death. . . .
>
> In this mysterious liturgy, the Church is overcome with immense grief. She remembers, She repeats in Her rites, She relives in Her feelings, the passion of Christ. She Herself is conscious of it, suffers from it, weeps at it. Do not disturb Her mourning, do not distract Her thought, do not mock Her remorse, do not consider Her anguish madness. You, too, surround the cry of Her pain with your silence; pity Her; honor Her with participation in Her noble spiritual affliction.

Thus the Holy Father described the spiritual, mystical, liturgical suffering of the Church—what one could call her compassion with Christ, her Bridegroom. But the suffering of the Church is not only liturgical, spiritual, mystical— "Lest the Cross of Christ be emptied of its power" (1 Cor. 1:17)—it is also real, as the dogmatic constitution on the

Church of Vativan II reminds us: "Just as Christ carried out the work of redemption in poverty and under oppression, so the Church is called to follow the same path in communicating to men the fruits of salvation" (*L.G.*, 8).

Pope Paul in this address drew attention to "the relationship there is between Christ suffering and His Church, between the Head and the Mystical Body, between the gospel of the passion of the Lord and the painful history of the Church." "The passion of the Lord," he continued, "is reflected in the Church. . . . It is somehow renewed, reproduced, repeated . . . not only in every individual follower of Christ . . . but in the whole Church, considered . . . as *His* life prolonged in history. It is perpetuated, and it is still going on."

"Is this so? Is the Church suffering today?" he asked. His answer leaves us in no doubt about the extent and the causes of the Church's suffering:

> Yes! The Church is undergoing great suffering . . . the Lord is testing us. The Church is suffering, as you know, from oppressive lack of legitimate freedom in so many countries of the world. She is suffering at the abandonment by so many Catholics of the fidelity that Her centuries-old tradition would deserve and Her pastoral effort, full of understanding and love, should obtain. She is suffering above all because of the restless, critical, unruly and destructive rebellion of so many of Her sons, Her dearest sons — priests, teachers, laymen . . . against Her institutional existence, against Her canon law, Her tradition, Her interior cohesion; against Her authority, the irreplaceable principle of truth, unity, charity; against Her very requirements of holiness and sacrifice; She is suffering at the defection and scandal of certain ecclesiastics and religious, who are crucifying the Church today.

In another address, of April 29, 1970, in answer to his opening question, "What is the Church doing?" he said: "The anxious query already contains the answer: The Church is suffering!" Once again he detailed the causes, both external and internal, and said: "We desire to consider the Church's suffering . . . as a fate which, in some respects, we might describe as normal, as something belonging naturally to its existence. That is how things are."

It is very evident that Pope Paul shares in a unique way in this suffering of the Church. On September 10, 1969, he said:

> That is how it is. How could the Pope and those who bear the responsibility of giving the Church pastoral guidance together with him not suffer as they see that the major difficulties are today arising out of the Church Herself, that the most poignant pain comes to Her from the indocility and the infidelity of certain of Her ministers and some of Her consecrated souls, that the most disappointing surprises come to Her from circles that have been the most assisted, the most favored and the most beloved? How can they not feel sorrow at the waste of so many energies?

It is also clear that he foresaw his role of suffering from the very occasion of his election as pope. On the ninth anniversary of his election he confided to those at the general audience of June 21, 1972, that he had written in his personal diary the following reflection on his election:

> Perhaps the Lord has called me to this service, not because of any aptitude of mine, not to govern and save the Church from Her present difficulties, but to suffer something for the Church, and to make it clear that He, and no one else, guides Her and saves Her.

Our own experiences of suffering, whether due to physical, psychological, or spiritual afflictions, should suffice to fill our hearts with sympathy and compassion for the Holy Father as he carries the cross with our divine Lord. But which of us can really say, no matter how grievous our burden may be, that we comprehend the extent and the height and the depth of the sufferings of this suffering pope? Do we, who are scandalized and saddened whenever we hear or read of yet another defection from the priestly or the religious state, really comprehend the burden placed by Christ on the shoulders of this frail and saintly vicar of his, who, on December 15, 1969, in an address responding to the Christmas greetings of the College of Cardinals, referred to the falling away of an "ever too noticeable number of priests and religious from their sacred duties" as his crown of thorns?

Indeed he lives, now not he, but Christ lives in him, and with Christ he is nailed to the cross, to paraphrase St. Paul

(Gal. 2:20). Have we nothing with which to reproach ourselves in the sufferings of the Church and of our Holy Fathers? Have we not, unwittingly perhaps, allied ourselves to those dissenters who see in the pope a sign of contradiction, when we ask, complainingly, what is he doing, tolerating such dissent and even open rebellion in the Church? Why doesn't he exercise the power of the keys? Is he not responsible, ultimately, for the crisis of authority, the crisis of confidence in the Church?

Pope Paul grasped this nettle during his address of September 10, 1969. "We hear much today," he told his audience, "of the troubles that are shaking the Church's life from the inside and have been doing so since the Council, in an unforeseen way that certainly does not derive from the Council itself through a logic of fidelity, but is even contrary to the Council's spirit, hopes and norms." So true is this, he noted, that some dare think and say that the council was insufficient and out of date.

> Generally speaking, we might call the present trouble a crisis of confidence . . . or rather a crisis of lack of confidence . . . in doctrine and a tradition . . . in structures and methods . . . in men . . . in the very acts of the renewal of the Church . . . in the Church as it is. Need we tell you that we ourself, and with us responsible persons and organs in the Church of God, are suspected of lack of confidence?

He referred to a remark made to him a few days previously by a great-minded churchman, which frankly stated that very suspicion and impression. "This remark made us think," said His Holiness: "Were we ourself overcome by loss of confidence?" He recalled Peter's weakness and vacillation, his confession that he was a sinner: "Depart from me, O Lord, for I am a sinful man" (Lk. 5:8), but also Peter's impassioned response to our Lord's question: "You know that I love you" (Jn. 21:15–17). The pope assured his audience that he has "all the interior certainty with which the Lord deigns to comfort our ministry."

He quoted St. Paul: "We carry this treasure in vessels of clay, to show that the abundance of the power is God's and not ours. In all things we suffer tribulation, but we are

not distressed; we are sore pressed, but we are not destitute"
(2 Cor. 4:7–8).

"Pain is one thing," he continued, "and loss of confidence
another. The grief which we can and do feel for the trials
of the Church at the present hour does not lessen our confidence in Her regard. Perhaps they even increase it, when
they oblige us to confide the Church so much more to the
Divine Wisdom, to Divine Aid. We let the Lord take us by
the hand and reproach us, 'O Thou of little Faith, why didst
Thou doubt?' (Mt. 14:31), and remind us to what unlikely
lengths we can take our confidence. . . . Christ is our hope,
our strength, and our peace."

He realized, he said, that many contestations arose in good
faith, out of concern for justice and for reform, out of reaction
to intolerable circumstances. He recalled the providential
function of certain ills that cause suffering, the fatal necessity
of even scandals in God's mysterious designs, and he expressed his conviction of the possibility of winning back every
human soul. He reposed his confidence on the knowledge
"that this postconciliar Church contains innumerable bands
of strong and faithful souls fervent in prayer . . . holy souls
. . . the Church's honor and joy . . . the strength of God's
people. They are our confidence."

And so when we ask "Why does Pope Paul not use the
power of the keys?" the answer is *he does*, in the way that he
has decided he should: by teaching, by confessing the faith,
by being the pastor and shepherd, by being "the intermediary
necessary for normal access to the Kingdom of Heaven." As
he told us, on the occasion of his election as pope, "Authority
and charity became, as in an inner vision, one thing; a thing
so great as to spread to the ends of the world, and to be extended to all the needs of mankind."

Therefore let us listen to his teaching, and when, as on
April 2, 1969, he begs, "Beloved sons, do not refuse us your
loyalty and your prayer," let us be counted among those who
respond wholeheartedly and with joy.

5. What Does It Mean to Be a Christian?

This is one of the fundamental questions, one that needs to be asked again and answered again in these days of "identity crises." We seem to be surrounded by people who do not know, or profess not to know, who they are or what they should be doing. Yet many of them still profess to be Christians.

How can this be? If we answer the question "What does it mean to be a Christian?" with the elementary, almost tautological statement, "The Christian is a follower of Christ," how can we explain the uncertainty about the Christian vocation that afflicts so many people today? Surely Christ, of all men, knew what he was about, and surely he left a blueprint for the Christian life for his followers? Alas, not so! we are told by some theologians. Christ at first did not know who he was or what it was he had to do. Only on the cross, they say, did he realize what was happening, and then he cried out: "My God, my God, why have You forsaken me?" What a travesty of the truth and the mystery of that reality of the atonement expressed so simply and profoundly by St. Paul in the phrase "He emptied Himself"!

It is no wonder that those who are enamored of such theological piffle should find themselves in, and should lead others into, such an existential fog as surrounds us at this point in history.

C. S. Lewis gave a series of radio broadcasts during World War II which he later published in book form under the title *Mere Christianity*. In the preface to the book he made a case for using "Christian" in its original, obvious meaning. He reminds the reader that the name "Christians" was first given at Antioch (Acts 11:26) to "the disciples," to those who accepted the teaching of the apostles. The book is very readable, very persuasive in its presentation of what Lewis called the common doctrines of Christianity. It has done an immense amount of good, but nowhere does it address the fundamental question: How do we know what was the authentic teaching of the apostles?

He refers to the Church as the "community of believers" and states that its common doctrines are those that have been, and still are, held by all who call themselves Christian, implying the criteria of St. Vincent of Lerins: *Quod semper, quod ubique, quod ab omnibus*—what has been believed always, everywhere, and by everyone.

It should be evident from our previous discussion that such a limited and incomplete vision of the Church and Christianity will not do. Catholic beliefs encompass all of Lewis's "mere" Christianity, *but very much more*. We can accept and enjoy the splendid-yet-threadbare tapestry woven by Lewis, but we know that we have a living artist—a corps of artists—continuously engaged in developing the full splendor of that tapestry of the faith. I refer to the living magisterium of the Church, and especially to him who is the artist-in-chief, the vicar of Christ on earth. What has he to say on such a momentous question? It was used as the title of an address he gave during a general audience on July 18, 1973, in which he posed the question and reflected on it.

The first thing we discover is that to be a Christian is to have a vocation, a call from God, an intentional call to the divine plan of salvation. "Consider your call, brethren," St. Paul wrote to the Corinthians (1 Cor. 1:26), and to the Ephesians he stated: "God chose us in Him [Christ] before the foundation of the world" (Eph. 1:4). And St. Peter wrote: "You are a chosen race, a royal priesthood, a holy nation, God's own people" (1 Pet. 2:9). So the pope tells us that "the first dawning awareness of our Christian conscience should be that of possessing an immense fortune, of being raised to an incomparable dignity."

Is it possible that the Holy Father is inciting us to pride, to vain conceit in our estate, to smug self-satisfaction as the predestined elect? No indeed. Our first reaction, of happiness and joy, is not only legitimate as a necessary element in Christian life, it is enhanced in the very expression of humility, in the disproportion between God's greatness and our littleness. "Remember the Magnificat of the Blessed Virgin," the pope bids us. *To be a Christian is to recognize the sublimity of our call by God and the joy that flows from it, which nothing should quench.*

Our awareness of this must lead to a fundamental obligation, namely, to give thanks to God and to worship him in the fullness of our new and supernatural identity. How do we do this? Above all in the sacrifice of the Mass and in reception of the Eucharist. This is the sacramental fulfillment of St. Paul's exclamation, "It is no longer I who live, but Christ who lives in me" (Gal. 2:20).

Is this all it means to be a Christian? Is this all the Holy Father had in mind when he reminded us of the exhortation of his predecessor, Pope St. Leo the Great: "O Christian, recognize your dignity"? Joy, praise, and worship in return for God's call to us? Surely this corresponds to our Lord's characterization of his yoke as sweet and his burden as light?

Of course it does. But the pope also recalled, in an address on October 1, 1969, the continuation of St. Leo's exhortation: "Do not fall back into the baseness of your old ways. Remember to what head, to what mystical body you belong. Think again, about how you were freed from the power of darkness, and have been carried across into the light of God's realm" (*Serm. 1 de Nat.*, pp. 54, 192).

And while urging every Christian to regain a lively and active awareness of his dignity, of what he has become through the marvelous, mysterious, real regeneration of baptism, namely, a son of God, penetrated by God's words, in fact a shrine of the Blessed Trinity, the Holy Father went on to say: "Do not lose your awareness of sin, your ability to judge between good and evil." The pope drew very practical advice from this fundamental admonition. We will return to this later, but for the moment I want to dwell on a more fundamental conclusion that is implied in his admonitions and in those of St. Leo the Great: *The Christian is also one who believes in the devil.*

On November 15, 1972, Pope Paul gave a very succinct account of the Catholic doctrine on the devil, after stating that one of the greatest needs of the Church today is defense from that evil which is called the devil, an evil which is contrasted with the beauty and goodness of God's creation, an evil which is "not merely a lack of something, but an effective agent, a living spiritual being, perverted and perverting: a terrible reality; mysterious and frightening."

"It is contrary to the teaching of the Bible and the Church," he declared, "to refuse to recognize the existence of such a reality," and he summarized the scriptural accounts of the devil's encounters with our divine Lord. It is clear from all the scriptural accounts that it is not a question of one devil but of many; he is legion. But there is a principal devil, whose name, Satan, means the adversary, the enemy—the secret enemy who sows errors and misfortunes in human history. He was "a murderer from the beginning . . . and the father of lies," as our Lord defined him (Jn. 8:44–45)—the "*mysterium iniquitatis*," in St. Paul's words (2 Thess. 2:3–12).

Pope Paul tells us we can assume the devil's sinister action where denial of God becomes radical, subtle, and absurd; where hypocritical and blatant lies assert themselves against evident truth; where love is extinguished by cold, cruel selfishness; where the name of Christ is impugned with willful and rebellious hatred; and where the spirit of the gospel is watered down and denied.

It is difficult indeed, at times, to discern the influence of the evil one, so subtle and sophisticated are his techniques. It is easier to state the remedies, the means of defense against such an enemy. They are, as always, prayer and fasting.

What, then, does it mean to be a Christian?

In addition to being a joyful, grateful, worshiping follower of Christ, an adoptive son of God, a shrine of the Blessed Trinity, *the Christian is one who is at war*—at war with "the baseness of his old ways," at war not "against flesh and blood but against the principalities and powers, against the world rulers of this present darkness, against the spiritual hosts of wickedness in the heavenly places" (Eph. 6:11–12).

Why is this? How can this be? Did not Christ, by his death on the cross, conquer death and, through death, sin? Did he not ransom us from the evil one with his blood?

Yes, all this is true—a great and consoling truth; indeed, salvific truth. But there is another truth we must face, a terrifying truth. Salvation is *offered* to us, but we must *accept* it, and in God's mysterious providence we must "work out our own salvation in fear and trembling" (Phil. 2:12).

So we have a profound paradox, a whole set of apparently contradictory hallmarks of the true Christian way of life. Joy and confidence side by side with fear and suffering; consciousness of the dignity of our state and the most profound humility; peace and war.

How can we reconcile such conflicting notions? Only in Christ! For what it means to be a Christian is to bear witness to Christ. This is the theme of the Second Vatican Council, notably in its dogmatic constitution on the Church, as Pope Paul reminded us in an address on January 10, 1968. To bear witness is to give testimony. Testimony is transmission of the Christian message by word of mouth, by example of life and works, even to the sacrifice of goods and well-being and life itself, if necessary.

To bear witness means we must know Christ. It is necessary in the divine plan of salvation, which depends, as it were, on a chain of testimony: first, our divine Lord himself, who gave testimony of the nature of God—Father, Son, and Holy Spirit—and of his plan of redemption; then the apostles, who were eyewitnesses and earwitnesses of Christ; then their successors in the Church, the pope and bishops in union with him, and priests and religious, all of us.

The end or purpose of the testimony is to produce faith.

The witness, the Christian, is a worker of faith; he is a witness for what the Church teaches, which is what Christ taught, "for there is no other name under heaven given to men whereby we must be saved" (Acts 4:12).

So it is only by referring to our Lord and his mission that we can resolve the seeming contradictions in the answers to our question, "What does it mean to be a Christian?"

Pope Paul brought this point out very forcefully in his address to a general audience on April 19, 1972, on the topic of joy and suffering in Christian life. "Thoughts, words, hearts are still drinking at the paschal fountain," he said, and noted that the real Christian cannot celebrate Easter only on Easter Sunday but *always*, because joy, the characteristic note of Easter, which springs from grace and charity, is also the dominant note, the dominant psychological expression, of the Christian character. "Rejoice in the Lord always, again I say rejoice," wrote St. Paul to the Philippians (Phil. 4:4, 3:1). "A Christian cannot be really sad, radically pessimistic," said Pope Paul, ". . . paschal joy is the style of Christian spirituality."

"But is not the Cross the sign of the Christian?" he continued. "Are we Christians not educated to a certain alliance with suffering? . . . And is not sacrifice the peak point of Christian greatness? . . . How are we to reconcile these two opposite expressions of Christian life, suffering and joy?"

The answer, though not easy, is evident. We are urged to accept suffering, but only to *exploit* it by merging it with the passion of our blessed Lord. The answer is evident in the drama of the paschal mystery, where justice and mercy meet, and death is swallowed up in life, and sorrow and joy are no longer inveterate enemies. In this mystery the evangelical message of the beatitudes finds its real meaning. "Blessed, in a future tomorrow, of which they have a foretaste even now, will be the poor, the hungry, the thirsty, the afflicted, the weeping poor." This is the proclamation of Jesus.

"On careful consideration in fact," the pope told us, "we see that in the faithful experience of Christian life the two moments, that of suffering and that of joy, can be superimposed and become simultaneous. . . . St. Paul could say 'with all our affliction, I am overjoyed' (2 Cor. 7:4). This is one of the most interesting and complex points of the psychology of the Christian, as if he lived a double life. *In fact he does—* his own human life, earthly life with all its adversities, and Christ's life which has already been infused into him." Thus the problem of reconciling opposites such as joy and suffering, confidence and fear, death and life has its only solution in the paschal mystery, in the Risen Savior.

It is in the paschal mystery also that we can find the answer to the problem of evil, which, as the pope reminds us, "remains one of the greatest and permanent problems for the human spirit, even after the victorious answer given by Jesus Christ." What is the answer to the problem of evil; what is our defense against the devil? The Holy Father answered: "Grace is the decisive defense. Innocence takes on the aspect of a fortress."

At first, this striking phrase seems just another expression of the Christian paradoxes. What could be less like a fortress than innocence? Is it not the very first line of defense against the attacks of Satan that we see crumbling on all sides—in our children, in ourselves, in womanhood, in the priestly and religious life, in the Church herself?

The pope followed this train of thought in his address of October 1, 1969, in which we find an almost brutally frank description of this paradoxical situation:

> The Church is proclaiming her vocation to sanctity, is renewing her missionary commitment, and declares herself to be a poor pilgrim on the road to higher, eschatological goals in God's Kingdom. On the other hand, she is also trying to adapt herself and assimilate herself to the world's ways; she is taking off her distinctive sacral garment for she wants to feel more human and earthly. . . . She is undergoing the world's changes and degradations with conformist, almost avant-garde zeal.

Can this be the vicar of Christ speaking, and describing the state of the Church in our time? Could this be what St. Paul meant when he said "I became all things to all men"?

The pope continued: "All think about the Church in terms of demagoguery and revolutionary violence, of religious demythologization, and especially in terms of acquiescence in the licence of shameless fashion, sexual passion, and spread of pornography."

Yes, it *is* the Holy Father speaking, describing the failure and the inadequacy of humanism, particularly in one aspect, which he sees as the gravest and most insidious danger to that human and Christian dignity we are bound to recognize and defend:

> It is the threat of an aggressive and epidemic eroticism expressing itself in unbridled, revolting, public and publicized ways. We find in this sad phenomenon the theory which opens the road to licence disguised as liberty, to aberrations of the instincts described as liberation from conventional scruples. Eroticism in promiscuity, pornographic representations of various kinds, then drugs. The senses are extolled, then brutalized. *They find abject expressions in ways which God's word has cursed.* Such eroticism is now assailing even the healthiest and most reserved circles, the family, the school, recreations. All defenses seem to be weakening and crumbling. It appears that in certain countries the law has come to give honorable treatment to every offense against human decency, against the sacrosanct right of innocence to be protected and the right of decency to be publicly respected. A sense of the inevitable seems to deter good and responsible people from rightful and effective action against all this.

We can begin to understand why the Holy Father said "innocence takes on the aspect of a fortress." It takes on such an aspect under the influence of grace which was merited for us by the passion and death of our divine Lord, but which must be acquired by us through faith and good works.

Faith alone will not do; as St. James said, "Faith without works is dead." Good works alone will not do, either. However lofty and seemingly noble the humanitarian ideals, motives, and actions of the man without faith, they are doomed to failure. Humanism fails in its efforts to achieve its aims; indeed it achieves the opposite, as in the pope's description of modern society. G. K. Chesterton put it very strikingly when he said, "If you take away the supernatural you are left with the unnatural."

Among good works, the most vital are prayer and fasting. Fasting includes not only ascetical but sacrificial effort, sacrifice of time, talent, and material resources. These must also be put at the disposal of innocence. *Innocence is not ignorance, but neither is it intimate knowledge of evil.* The pope warns us not to be misled into thinking that knowledge of evil has to be acquired through personal experience. This is a temptation to which the Evil One constantly has resort— which worked very well for him with Eve. *The symbolic meaning of the tree of the knowledge of good and evil must never be lost sight of.* It is the temptation of those who maintain that formal classroom instruction in the mechanics of sexual behavior, including all its abervations, is necessary to protect children from misuse of sex, and that education in the forms, means, and results of drug abuse is vital in the crusade against drug abuse. What fools! All such programs have led, and inevitably lead, to an exponential increase in the very evils they are supposed to remedy.

We must also be vigilant even in morally acceptable educational programs, such as the movement to educate people about natural family planning. Laudable though its goal may be, of informing couples that there are morally licit and effective means of spacing births, or even of avoiding procreation entirely, if sufficiently grave reasons for doing so exist, one must call attention to the fact that *morally neutral or morally licit means may be used to produce an immoral result.*

We cannot forget that the Christian is continually tempted by the Father of Lies to either Manicheism or Pelagianism, and either heresy can lead to the antilife mentality that sees pregnancy as a disease, to be avoided like the plague. It doesn't matter if this mentality is fostered and made possible by artificial contraception or by symptothermal recognition of fertile cycles. So the pope bids us recall the virtues on which Christian mentality and life depend for their growth.

> Do not call purity and self-control ignorance and weakness. . . . Do not think that some inferiority complex lies behind frank and dignified defense of decency in the press, in shows, in social life and habits. . . . Give to ascetic effort, heroic sacrifice, and love of the brethren the importance which Christ, the Crucified Redeemer, gave them.
>
> "Remember, O Christian, your dignity," wrote St. Leo the Great.

"Have courage," said Our Blessed Lord, "for I have overcome the world."

The addresses presented in this chapter are but a sampling of many in which we find the Holy Father wrestling with the problem of this paradox of Christianity: the contrast between the ineffable reality of the gratuitous gift of God, the faith, with its joy, peace, serenity, charity, and sure conviction of ultimate success, and the harsh realities of our temporal existence. He devotes his attention now to one, then to the other. Thus on May 24, 1972, he drew from his reflections on the Feast of Pentecost a marvelous summary statement on the role of the Holy Spirit in the genesis of the supernatural life and in the unity of the Church, the mystical body of Christ, as well as in her incessant urge to bear witness "to the truth, about God, Christ, and the Gospel." He reminds us that *the Christian vocation is by its very nature also a vocation to the apostolate*, as stated so emphatically in the Second Vatican Council's documents, for example, in the decree on the laity (*Apost. Actuos.*, 2 and 5). So to the answers already given to our question "What does it mean to be a Christian?" we have to add: "To be a Christian means to be an apostle," in a real though nonhierarchical sense.

Almost immediately the Holy Father turned to what it takes to carry out this apostolate:

> The Christian, the Apostle, especially, is obliged to be strong and courageous, to be frank and free, as becomes a follower of Christ. But there always exists, even in the most committed (We are thinking, alas! of Peter . . .), an incurable frailty . . . which overwhelms us with . . . self-consciousness, conformity with fashion, paralyzing fear of the judgment or irony of others or of the press. . . . As Pascal remarked, "Public opinion wears one down" (*Pensees,* n. 303).
>
> [Christianity takes real courage.] First of all [said Pope Paul in his address of August 8, 1973], because the following of Christ has always called for this realistic vision and this inward courage. "Not everyone who says to Me, Lord, Lord, shall enter the Kingdom of Heaven, but he who does the will of My Father Who is in Heaven" (Mt. 7:21); and again, "Enter by the narrow gate . . . for the gate is narrow and the way is hard that leads to life . . ."; "If any man would come after Me, let him deny himself and take up his cross and follow Me. For

whoever would save his life will lose it, and whoever loses his life for My sake will find it" (Mt. 16:24–25).

These are hard sayings, but they are Christ's words. We may turn a deaf ear to them and, like those disciples who found other sayings of his preposterous, we may walk no more with him. But if we wish to follow him, to be Christian, we have no option but to listen to and heed *all* his sayings.

Of all his "hard" sayings, none seems more incredible, more impossible of achievement, than that recorded by St. Matthew, "You, therefore, must be perfect, as your heavenly Father is perfect" (Mt. 5:48). We may well ask, as the Holy Father did in an address on June 14, 1972, "Is it possible that so much is asked of us?"

Is this the final answer to our question "What does it mean to be a Christian"? If so, where are the Christians? Let us not fool ourselves! Let us take the beam out of our own eye and forget the mote in the other's eye. The question is directed at us, at you, at me! Not at the waffling theologian, the weak bishop, the avant-garde catechist, the secularized sister. The pope says

> there are many mediocre Christians, not just because they are weak or lack formation, but *because they want to be mediocre,* and because they have their good reasons — "the happy mean," . . . "the freedom of the Gospel," as if the Gospel were a school of moral indolence, or as if it authorized the ambiguity of serving two or more masters. . . . Is this not hypocrisy, inconsistency, relativism according to which way the wind blows? *Is it not taking the cross out of Christianity?*

The Holy Father pursued the question "What is this holiness of which we are speaking? What is this perfection?" He provided the same answer that we find everywhere in Scripture and everywhere in the authentic teachings of the Church. It is a double answer, for there are two components in holiness: *the grace of the Holy Spirit and our "yes," our submission to that power.* "The meeting of God's loving and saving will with the obedient and happy will of our human heart is perfection, holiness. The young usually understand the truth, the beauty, the vocation of this meeting, placed at the summit of a stupendous tension."

Did not our divine Lord tell us the same thing when he said "Let the little children come to Me, and do not hinder them, for of such is the Kingdom of God. Amen I say to you, whoever does not accept the Kingdom of God as a little child will not enter into it" (Lk. 18:16–17)?

So we can understand, as we read in the history of Eusebius of Caesarea, why the father of Origen, Leonidas, in thanking God for the gift of this son, the first of his seven children, bent over to kiss his breast as the boy lay sleeping. *He believed, you see, that the Holy Spirit dwelled there* (Eusebius, *Hist. Eccl.*, 1, VI, C. II, 11). This charming story of the simple yet profound faith of Leonidas, the blessed martyr, brings us back to that striking statement of Pope Paul on April 19, 1972: *"Grace is the decisive defense* [against the devil]. *Innocence takes on the aspect of a fortress."*

We can perhaps understand that phrase better now. The innocence of the child, Origen, which merited the reverence of his father, is but a faint reflection, an image, of the innocence of the child Jesus. The innocence of Jesus in his human nature, as a child and as a man, is a result of the incarnation, by which the fullness of the Godhead dwelt in him.

If we are to call ourselves Christian, we must believe in the divinity of Christ. The very first general council of the Church was called in defense of that fundamental belief against the Arians.

If we are Christians, we must also believe firmly in Christ's full humanity. The Church has rallied many times in defense of that belief also, and we find it emphasized by C. S. Lewis as a central tenet of his "mere" Christianity.

It is in reference to His human nature that we can speak of the innocence of Jesus. And it is because God came on earth in that human nature to reveal his triune divine nature and to atone for the primal sin of our first parents, ransoming us at a great price, that we see the innocence of Jesus in every Christian soul. This innocence of our divine Savior is reflected in every person who bears his name and believes in him as God-made-man. It is this innocence which, the Holy Father assures us, takes on the aspect of a fortress.

In a little book describing his reactions to the International

Eucharistic Congress in Dublin in 1932, G. K. Chesterton made it clear that the Son of God-made-man was everywhere in Dublin that week, as he is every day and every place in the world where the Mass is said and the sacrament confected. He was surely a real presence and a real person to the very poor, very threadbare working woman who was heard to say, as the fine summer weather threatened to break, "Well, if it rains now, He will have brought it on Himself!"

For Chesterton, this remark and the possibility that evoked it—that the eucharistic events might be drowned in thunderstorms—were an expression, verbal and symbolic, of a most profound truth that stands almost like a contradiction at the heart of the Christian mystery: the God without, seeming to sacrifice the God within; the very world of the Creator turned against the unworldliness of the Crucified; the Father accepting the death of the Son. The remark might very well have been made by Caiaphas or Pilate, he thought; for indeed He *does* rather have a way of bringing it on himself!

Chesterton's further reflections on the reported remark and its circumstances led to profound and unusual but very characteristic insights into the central core of the Christian mystery, the incarnation, and into man's reactions to it in the course of history. He recalled the violent denial of the Jews and Moslems, in the very places of the birth, ministry, and salvific death of Christ. He commented on the Monophysites, who simplified the God-man by saying he is only God, and on the simplicity of the Modernists who insist he was only man. It led him to the insight that the genius of the Church and the true faith, wherever and whenever it is found, is to maintain the essential perspective on the essential paradox of the incarnation, *the doctrine of the double nature of Christ. This is what it means to be a Christian.*

It led him also to another insight, into how this perspective is maintained: *simply by keeping in mind the Mother of Christ.*

Chesterton remembered a legend he had heard in Ireland many years before the congress—that someone in a wild and lonely place had met a beautiful peasant woman carrying a child. On being asked her name, she had answered simply:

"I am the Mother of God, and this is Himself, and He is the Boy you will all be wanting at the last."

Legend it may be, but it expresses in the language of a simple, natural literature the spirit and the significance of that doctrine that is at the very heart of Christianity: *belief in the fullness of the manhood of Jesus Christ, with which dwelt the fullness of the Godhead, bodily.*

This is what it means to be a Christian.

6. The Seriousness of Our Claim to be Catholics

The discussion of Pope Paul's answers, and ours, to the question "What does it mean to be a Christian?" has led us to a number of fundamental conclusions, some of them at first sight paradoxical, all of them challenging.

First, to be a Christian means to believe in God—a personal God, almighty, all knowing, all loving—God one in three, Father, Son, and Holy Spirit.

Secondly, to be a Christian means to believe in the incarnation—to believe that the Second Person of the Blessed Trinity entered into the world, created by God at a finite moment in its history, and assumed a human nature. We argued that this very specific and unique belief of Christians meant that the baby born to the Virgin Mary was both divine and human; he was one Person with two natures. We affirmed that authentic Christianity demands that we believe in the full divinity and in the full humanity of Christ, without ever losing sight of either. Because of this fundamental truth, Mary is Mother of God; she is *Theotokos*, as the Greeks said.

We saw that to be a Christian means to believe in the devil and in the fall of Adam and Eve from their state of original justice—that fall which was the first paradox in

God's dealings with his human creatures, that fall which the Church, in the exuberance of her paschal joy, addresses as *"O felix Culpa, quae talem ac tantum meruit Redemptorem!"*

We found that Christianity means to believe that God's purposes in sending his only-begotten Son into the world are (1) to reveal to us something of his own intimate divine nature: that three of his most characteristic attributes are creative omnipotence, creative wisdom, and creative love—attributes of three persons, Father, Son, and Holy Spirit in one Godhead; (2) to redeem us from the bondage of sin and the devil through the passion and death of Jesus Christ, the God-man; and (3) to give us the opportunity, once more, through the power of the Holy Spirit, to be formed in his image, now manifest to us in the face, person, and life of Christ, his divine Son, our brother.

We dwelt at some length on the extraordinary contrasts in the life and actions of our Savior: his meekness and his sternness, his loving forgiveness of repentant sinners and his fierce condemnations of hypocrites and scandal givers; his shameful death and his resurrection; and we saw that to be a Christion means to be forever trying to reconcile seeming contradictions in our own lives, such as joy and suffering, innocent weakness and the power of the Spirit, peace and war.

In our discussion we alluded to the fact that to be a Christian means a great deal more than adherence to what C. S. Lewis called the common doctrines of Christianity. It can be said that most of these beliefs are held by many of our separated brethren, and frequently with much better practical results in their lives than we exhibit, despite our possession of the fullness of the faith. As Monsignor John O'Connor, pastor of St. Cuthbert's Church in Bradford, Yorkshire, and model for G. K. Chesterton's Father Brown, remarked: "Protestants are so much better than their faith warrants, and Catholics so seldom live up to theirs!"

So it is fitting that we should question ourselves, as the Holy Father did on July 11, 1973, on the seriousness of our claim to be Catholics, on measuring that claim in the overwhelming context of modern life, specifying the influence that our Christian profession has on our lives. The pope asks:

"Are we still believers? Is our Christian vocation still the decisive fact for us? Or are we survivors in a weary, fragmentary ecclesial tradition?"

Before we can ask or attempt to answer these questions, we must establish what we profess. To put it another way, is there such a thing as *Catholic* Christianity? If so, how is it distinguished from "mere Christianity"? On our answers will depend our response to the other question implied in our title, namely, "the seriousness of our claim to be Catholics." For if Christianity be "mere Christianity," then our yardstick for judgment will be our fidelity to the written word of God; but if, as we said, it is very much more, we must establish what separates us from our separated brethren. It is by these criteria, not theirs, that we must judge the seriousness of our claim to be Catholics.

In the preface to his book *Mere Christianity*, Lewis refers to his reasons for saying no more about the Blessed Virgin Mary than is involved in asserting the virgin birth of Christ:

> To say more would take me at once into highly controversial regions. And there is no controversy between Christians which needs to be so delicately touched as this. The Roman Catholic beliefs on that subject are held not only with the ordinary fervor that attaches to all sincere religious beliefs, but (very naturally) with the peculiar and, as it were, chivalrous sensibility that a man feels when the honor of his mother or his beloved is at stake. It is very difficult so to dissent from them that you will not appear to them a cad as well as a heretic. And contrariwise, the opposed Protestant beliefs on this subject call forth feelings which go down to the very roots of all monotheism whatever. To radical Protestants it seems that the distinction between Creator and creature (however holy) is imperilled: that polytheism is risen again. Hence it is hard so to dissent from them that you will not appear something worse than a heretic — an idolator, a pagan.

But we have already said, and it is *de fide Catholica*, that Mary is the Mother of God, *Theotokos*, and it is evident that many of Lewis's fellow Anglicans, as well as Christians of other denominations, are coming closer to, if they have not already accepted, that fundamental belief.

We believe that the Mother of God is our Mother also

and that, as declared by *Lumen Gentium* of Vatican II and by Pope Paul VI, she is the Mother of the Church.

From all this we can deduce the conclusion that one major test of the seriousness of our claim to be Catholics must be our attitude toward the Blessed Mother. Our fervor or lukewarmness for her is precisely the degree of our commitment to her divine Son-made-man, the measure of the seriousness of our claim to be Catholics.

But we have another and, in the practical order, more reliable standard for judging ourselves as Catholics. We know full well what that standard is; it is, as Pope Paul never tires of reminding us, *our fidelity to the Church.* In an address on August 14, 1968, he asked his audience: "Is there an existential difference between the person who is a Christian and the one who is not?" "Certainly," he answered, "there *is* a difference which strongly characterizes the Christian." His statement of what makes this difference is quite removed from Lewis's *Mere Christianity:*

> This Christian character, this spiritual imprint . . . is stamped indelibly by three sacraments on the soul of those who receive them . . . Baptism . . . Confirmation . . . Ordination to the priesthood. [He went on to speak of this "stupendous anthropology," of the sublimity of the state of grace which qualifies it, and of the necessity of the sacraments to establish, nourish, and, if necessary, re-establish it.] The mystery of salvation is communicated to us in two ways: by the Word of God and by sacramental action. To these ways there is a third that we may add, the Church — *that great sacrament containing and dispensing the others,* which gives our lives the Christian style, offering us the atmosphere of the Spirit whose soul she is, and which, if we are faithful, she will let us breathe.

When we examine, in a later chapter, the question "What Church did Jesus Christ actually found?" we will learn much about the ecclesiology of Pope Paul, but it seems to me that if the essentials of his teaching about the Church had to be summed up in one sentence, the one I have just quoted would be difficult to discard. The Church is a "great sacrament," the "third way" of communicating to us the mystery of salvation, which contains and dispenses the other two: the Word of God and sacramental action. It is because of this truth that we owe undying fidelity to the Church, not the "Church of the first century" or the Church of any century, but the *living* Church, the infallible custodian and interpreter of the mind of Christ.

The need for such an infallible interpreter is underscored time and again by Pope Paul. He is obviously, and frequently, preoccupied with the difficulty (as he put it on December 4, 1968) of "translating religious truths into understandable words, of preserving the inviolable orthodoxy of the Christian dogma and clothing it in a language accessible to the men of our time." He alluded in this address to the multiple forms of study and theological exposition that characterize the efforts at adaptation, *aggiornamento*—efforts that have led to "the not infrequent inaccuracy of ecclesiastical and Catholic utterances both written and spoken." He is obviously concerned to defend and delimit the relative freedom of study and exposition of scholars and teachers, so much so that he has been accused of Modernist leanings!

Nothing could be further from the truth. He constantly reiterates the central and essential disposition which identifies the authentic loyal Catholic among all his Christian brethren, that disposition which enables him *"sentire cum ecclesia."* It is the disposition *to hold fast to the supreme magisterium.* In this same address of December 4, 1968, the pope said:

> This effort to adapt the revealed Word to the understanding of listeners . . . is exposed to the danger of going beyond the intention that makes it praiseworthy . . . the danger of ambiguity, reticence or distortion of the message. It may even be led into the temptation of choosing among the treasure of revealed truths the ones that are popular, leaving out the others, or the temptation of shaping these truths in accordance with arbitrary and particular conceptions. . . . *This is a danger and a temptation to which everyone is exposed, because everyone, coming into contact with the Word of God, tries to adapt it to his own mentality, his own culture.*

This temptation has resulted, as we know, in the fragmentation of Christianity. Why is this so? Has not the Church always adapted herself to every age and culture? Yes, the answer is precisely yes! *It is the Church that can adapt her-*

self, not her individual members. What the Holy Father is speaking about, he makes plain, is

> that free examination which takes away from this same Word of God its univocal significance and its objective authority, and ends up by depriving the community of believers of adhesion to an identical truth, to the same faith. The "one faith" disintegrates and with it that very community that is called the one, true Church. This should be enough to convince us that the Divine Plan is right in wishing the revealed Word, contained in the Scriptures and in the apostolic tradition, to be protected by a vehicle of transmission. *We mean a visible and permanent Magisterium, authorized to guard, interpret, teach that Word. . . .* One condition is necessary: *respect for the integrity of the revealed message.* As you know, the Catholic Church is jealous, severe, exacting and dogmatic on that point. *The formulas in which doctrine was defined, after thought and with authority, cannot be abandoned.* The Church's Magisterium makes us conscious in this regard even at the cost of having to bear the negative consequences of her doctrine having an unpopular appearance. *The Magisterium cannot do otherwise.*

In a very forceful address on January 21, 1970, in which he spoke of the week of prayer for unity and of the Christian's fundamental duty to preserve unity, Pope Paul gave a concise summary of the essential history of fragmentation of that unity and of the seemingly insurmountable difficulties in the restoration of what the Church essentially is, communion. "Ecumenism," he said, "seems to be wearing itself out in an illusory effort!" He then made a somewhat unexpected comment—unexpected in the rosy flush of ecumenism and irenicism that suffused the immediate postconciliar period:

> One reason for this lies in the generous attempts which modern *non-Catholic* ecumenism is making. *It has to acknowledge the particular belief of each Christian denomination;* it does indeed arouse and stimulate the problem of unity, *yet it cannot solve that problem without the authority and the charism of unity which we hold to be Peter's divine prerogative.*
> But, some say, could not Peter drop his numerous demands? Could not Catholics and dissidents celebrate together the highest and most definitive act of the Christian religion, the Eucharist? Could they not then proclaim that the longed-for unity had at last been attained?

> Unfortunately, no! Unity cannot be achieved by a *fait accompli,* by intercommunion, as they say. How could there be unity without the same faith, without the same valid priesthood?

Nevertheless, the Holy Father sounded an optimistic note, while warning of vain and harmful, unauthorized, and conformist attempts to obtain false unity. And when he asked his audience "What can we do to shorten the way, to make it easier?" he answered his question as follows: "We must all examine our own consciences!" For what purpose, you may ask—to accuse ourselves of sins against ecumenism, of a false irenicism?

> One response is general and valid for all [the pope said]. Let us try to be true Catholics. Convinced Catholics! Firm Catholics! Good Catholics! *There cannot be a watered down, approximate and camouflaged Catholicism,* still less if it implies denying by our behavior what will bring ourselves and our separated brethren mutually closer.
>
> *A religious and moral aping of easier and questionable forms of the Christian life will not help our witness or apostleship,* nor will it gain anything by way of esteem, example and trust. *It will serve only to depreciate the cause of Christ and His Church.*

He pointed to the council's relevant teaching that "all Catholics ought to strive for Christian perfection" so that the attraction toward unity of the Church may be effective, and he concluded with a list of the virtues necessary to that end: unity and fraternal charity among Catholics, firmness and simplicity of faith, humility (because of the gift of that full and true faith), open and generous kindness to all, the spirit of service and sacrifice, love for Christ crucified and risen, and, of course, prayer, since the undertaking is so far beyond our strength.

Pope Paul speaks repeatedly of the Church as custodian, transmitter, and interpreter of the doctrines of faith. We shall deal with his teachings on the Church more systematically and completely in a later chapter, but three of what might be called his ecclesiologic addresses are very pertinent to our judgment of the seriousness of our claim to be Catholics.

The first of these, in logical order though not in chronological sequence, was made on January 19, 1972. It begins in a poetic vein, describing man discovering himself in the darkness of cosmic questions, illuminated by the Christian fact, as if the well-known words of St. John's gospel had been uttered at that every moment: "The light shines in the darkness" (Jn. 1:5). Man discovers himself as the privileged wayfarer, advancing, tiny and supreme, over the world stage and capable of transcending it even as he can dominate it, transcending it in the fascination of a new relationship that is superior to him: a dialogue with God which opens in this way, "Our Father who art in heaven . . ."

It is not a dream, or a hallucination, or an overexcited imagination. It is simply the effect of a light shining on a soul which has opened to its rays. The light is called revelation; the opening of the soul is called faith.

The Holy Father came to grips with the question of on-going revelation in the same breath as he dealt with the divine origin of revelation:

> Is contact with God resulting from the Gospel a moment of natural evolution of the human spirit, an evolution that still continues . . . or is it a single definitive moment on which we must nourish ourselves endlessly, but always recognizing its essential content as unchangeable?
>
> The answer is clear: it is a single and definitive moment. *Revelation is inserted in time, in history, at a precise date, on the occasion of a specific event, and it must be regarded as concluded and complete for us with the death of the Apostles.* Revelation is a fact, an event, and at the same time a mystery, which did not have its origin in the human spirit, but came from a Divine intervention. It had many progressive manifestations, spread out over a long history, the Old Testament; and it culminated in Jesus Christ. *Thus for us eventually the Word of God is the Word Incarnate, the historical Christ, who continues to live in the community united with Him through faith and the Holy Spirit, in the Church which is His Mystical Body.*
>
> *This is how things are,* beloved sons; *and in this way our doctrine is separated from the errors which have circulated and still crop up in the culture of our times,* and which might ruin completely our Christian conception of life and history. Modernism was the characteristic expression of these errors, *and it still exists today,* under other names.
>
> So we can understand why the Catholic Church, in the

> past and today, has given and gives so much importance
> to the scrupulous preservation of the authentic revela-
> tion. She considers it an inviolable treasure, and is stern-
> ly aware of her fundamental duty to defend and transmit
> the doctrine of the faith in unequivocal terms. Ortho-
> doxy is her first concern; the pastoral magisterium her
> primary and providential function. *The apostolic teach-
> ing fixed the canons of her preaching.*
>
> The Apostle Paul's order to Timothy, *"Depositum cus-
> todi!"* (1 Tim. 6:20; 2 Tim. 1:16) is for her such a
> commitment that it would be a betrayal to violate it.
> *The teaching Church does not invent her doctrine*; she
> is a witness, a custodian, an interpreter, a transmitter.
> As regards the truths of the Christian message, she can
> be called conservative, uncompromising. To those who
> urge her to make her faith easier, more in keeping with
> the tastes of the changing mentality of the times, she
> answers with the Apostle's *"Non possumus,* we cannot!"
> (Acts 4:20).

It is evident from the foregoing that Pope Paul is no waffling theologian but a clear and firm expositor of what fundamentally characterizes the Catholic, namely, adherence to
the faith handed down to us from the apostles and conserved,
developed, and expounded by the successors of those apostles,
the bishop of Rome, and all those bishops in communion with
him.

Pope Paul was even more forthright and explicit in the
apostolic exhortation issued in 1970 on the fifth anniversary
of the close of the Second Vatican Council. Directed "to all
the Bishops in peace and communion with the Holy See," it
reminded them of the fundamental essentials of their duties
and their rights. It reminded them of the benefits they had
derived from the recent council and of the commitment they
had made at the very outset of the council: "to take pains
to so present to the men of this age God's truth in its integrity and purity that they may understand it and gladly
assent to it"—a commitment made even more explicit in the
pastoral constitution *Gaudium et Spes:* "She [the Church]
intends to propose to our age over and over again, in season
and out of season, the Apostolic message."

The pope pointed out that the shepherds of the Church have
always had this duty of transmitting the faith in its fullness
and in a manner suited to men of their time. For "it is in

fact the Episcopal College which *with Peter, and under his authority*, guarantees the authentic handing on of the deposit of faith, and for that purpose it has received, as St. Irenaeus expressed it, 'a sure charism of truth.' " He reminded them of the words of *Lumen Gentium*:

> Bishops, teaching in communion with the Roman Pontiff, are to be respected by all as witnesses to Divine and Catholic truth. In matters of faith and morals, the Bishops speak in the name of Christ and the faithful are to accept their teaching and adhere to it with a religious assent [*L.G.*, 25].

From this he drew the practical conclusion that "the teaching office of the Bishops is for the believer the sign and channel which enable him to receive and recognize the Word of God."

What does this practical rule mean for us? It means that we must presume that the bishop of the diocese in which we live is in tune with the supreme magisterium of the Church, and we need to be very sure of ourselves and of the facts before we come to the opposite conclusion, namely, that he is no longer "the sign and channel" referred to by the Holy Father.

The pope, however, does not allow the bishops to hide, as it were, behind the speculations of theologians. He was in this exhortation, as in so many of his addresses, very emphatic and explicit in stating the place and the role of theologians in the Church. For instance, he quoted with approval the declaration of the German bishops, made in 1968, which stated:

> Theology, being the science of the faith, can only find its norm in the Church, the community of the believers. *When theology rejects its postulates and understands its norm in a different way, it loses its basis and its object. The religious freedom affirmed by the Council,* and which rests upon freedom of conscience, is valid for the personal decision in relation to faith, *but it has nothing to do with determining the content and scope of Divine Revelation.*

To this important, indeed vital statement, Pope Paul added, "In like manner, the utilization of human scientific knowledge in research in hermeneutics is a way of investigating the revealed data, but these data cannot be reduced to the analyses thus provided, because they transcend them both in origin and content." With these statements we are clearly liberated from the bondage of the experts! But perhaps there is still some doubt in one's mind about the danger of unfettered expertise, or perhaps one will still be intimidated if and when a bishop defends a faulty teaching by saying, "But the theologians and Scripture scholars tell us, etc., etc."

I beg you to listen to and remember these words of Pope Paul in the same apostolic exhortation:

> In face of the ravages being inflicted upon the Christian people by the diffusion of venturesome hypotheses or opinions that disturb faith, we have the duty to recall, with the Council, that true theology "rests upon the written Word of God, together with sacred tradition, as its perpetual foundation" (*Dei Verb.*, 24).
>
> Let us not be reduced to silence for fear of criticism . . . however necessary the function of theologians, it is not to the learned that God has confided the duty of authentically interpreting the faith of the Church: that faith is borne by the life of the people whose bishops are responsible for them before God. *It is for the bishops to tell the people what God asks them to believe.*

This insistence by the pope on the power and authority of the bishops who are in communion with him falls on many deaf ears, as we well know. It is contested in the very name of that council whose teachings, as we have seen, Pope Paul has made his own. The council, the dissidents say, put an end to this outmoded concept of a hierarchical authoritarian Church; the Church is a people, God's people, they say, quoting *Lumen Gentium*. The Church is a communion. Did not our Lord himself say at the Last Supper, "Let him who rules be as a servant" (Lk. 22:26)? And they quote with approval Alexander Manzoni's statement, in reference to Cardinal Borromeo as the ideal bishop, "There is no just superiority of one man over other men unless it be to serve them" (*The Betrothed*, ch. 22). And so authority is service, and authority is at the service of the people of God: the people are the Church!

Pope Paul dealt with this deviation in an address on November 12, 1969, speaking of what he called a number of

pseudo concepts. He agreed that authority is service and recalled that Pope St. Gregory the Great's description of himself as servant of the servants of God is still one of the pope's
titles.

> It is [he said] a precise, meaningful and monitory for-
> mula; *but it does not annul the Pope's power.* Like every
> other similar formula referring to legitimate authority,
> authority in the Church is *for* service of the brethren:
> It is not *at* someone else's service [i.e., at the beck and
> call of the brethren]. In other words, the purpose of
> authority is the good of others. *It does not mean that
> others are the source of the authority itself* . . . the
> Church . . . does not derive her power from below; she
> derives it from Christ, from God, and is responsible only
> to Him.

And so the authentic vision of the Church is that of a
hierarchical communion. The description of the Church as
the people of God needs to be completed, with that of the
Church as the mystical body of Christ—an organic society
with different charisms, differing functions, differing responsibilities. We must not be carried away by the lively
consciousness of our liberty and personality, of our dignity as
sons of God.

> Indeed [the Holy Father reminds us], the more we
> feel that we are self-sufficient units, capable of deciding
> for ourselves and about ourselves and responsible for
> ourselves, the more we should at the same time remain
> aware that we are in a community and hierarchical order.
> These two develop together and aid each other.
> This is what it means to be Catholic: united and
> universal. We live the mystery of the hierarchical com-
> munion in this acquired fullness of our personalities by
> remaining attached to the order which objectively ac-
> knowledges that communion and transcends it, that is
> by remaining attached to obedience to God's will, even,
> indeed especially, when it is made known to us through
> a brother who is authorized to be its intermediary.
> This is to say that we "live" the Church, and reflect
> Christ's mystery in ourselves. [In this sense the people
> are the Church.] His human life was totally dominated
> by conscious and heroic loyalty to the Father's will —
> *factus obediens usque ad mortem* (Phil. 2:5–8; Jn. 6:38).

The Holy Father is telling us that the seriousness of our
claim to be Catholics is to be judged by the evidence—the
evidence of our attachment to obedience to God's will. The

divine will is made known to us not by special revelation but through the teaching authority he has established in his Church, through the pope and bishops who are in communion with Him. In the last analysis, we can judge the seriousness of our claim to be Catholics only by the seriousness of our claim to be "Papists," the pope's loyal sons and daughters. I do not mean minimalists—those who accept only *de fide* statements—but those who were spoken of by the Second Vatican Council, who sincerely adhere to the judgments made by the pope according to his manifest mind and will, even when he is not speaking *ex cathedra*.

7. Pope Paul, Man of Faith

"By the power of God you are guarded through faith for salvation" (1 Pet. 1:5).

These words were written by the first vicar of Christ on earth, St. Peter, in his first epistle. Toward the end of that letter he reminded the early Christians, and us, that the adversary, the devil, was going about like a roaring lion seeking someone to devour. "Resist him," he urged, "strong in the Faith!" (1 Pet. 5:9).

How little things have changed since that year of A.D. 63, when the letter was written to the Christian communities of Asia Minor, which were being tested in the fire, as Peter said!

In the year that followed, the great persecution of the Church by Nero was to begin, and Peter's own final testing was not far off. From his prison cell he sent the same Christians his second epistle, occasioned by the appearance among them of false teachers, heretics, and deceivers, who seemingly had used the theological complexities of St. Paul's writings to support their errors. In these epistles of St. Paul, said Peter, are "certain things difficult to understand, which the unlearned and the unstable distort, just as they do the rest of the Scriptures also, to their own destruction" (2 Pet. 3:16).

How like our own times! Everywhere today the city of God, the Church, is under siege, by neo-pagan hordes and false philosophies, while within the very walls there is a Trojan horse, as von Hildebrand has written.

Peter's successor, Pope Paul VI, calls attention in his addresses and writings again and again to the very same problems that concerned St. Peter. Thus on August 1, 1973, he asked his audience to consider some of the difficulties besetting the faith in modern times: on one hand a secular, rationalistic, materialistic, empirical culture and mentality that rejects supernatural faith and, on the other, what he called a many-sided obstacle which had arisen in biblical studies. This, he said,

> claimed the right, with the aid of subtle and expert erudition, to submit Holy Scripture, the Gospels especially, to an exegesis, a new and destructive interpretation, by means of specious but questionable principles, in order to deprive the Sacred Book of its genuine authority, the authority that the Church recognizes it as having and which makes it the subject and object of Traditional Faith.

The words are different from St. Peter's but the problem is the same. And the answer to it, given by the vicar of Christ in this twentieth century, does not differ from that given by him of the first century. "We are not afraid," said the pope; "Faith has been subject to innumerable and continual attacks in the course of history. . . . Let us all try to be 'strong in faith' (1 Pet. 5:9) as St. Peter exhorts us!"

But what is faith? We need to return to this question again and again, as the pope does, and reflect on the richness of meaning of the answers he provides. "The Church needs Faith . . . Faith is the first need of the Church . . . rather, an *increase of Faith* seems to us the first and great need of the Church today; and this is a need which each of us can put right." So said Pope Paul on September 27, 1972.

"Faith is the root of our religion," he told us; "it is the original bond knitting us together to form the Church." This is true, of course, but what of those who are not members of the visible Church? Is faith impossible for them? By no means! All men are called to faith. "*Justus ex fide vivit*, the just man lives by Faith," St. Paul wrote to the Galatians (3:11), to the Hebrews (10:38), and to the Romans (1:17), but he was simply repeating the words of the prophet Habacuc (Hab. 2:4).

St. Paul's namesake, Pope Paul, echoed this same statement of fact in many of his addresses, largely in the context
of the faith as a rule of life. But in an address on June 12,
1968, he spoke of faith in its *primary* meaning of *natural
knowledge of God*, that is, knowledge of the Divinity which
can be had through our ordinary powers of thought. "We
maintain," he said, "that this is a basic truth," recalling that
it has been *de fide* since the First Vatican Council. In the
decree *Dei Filius* we find a summary of the age-long doctrine
of the Church and the affirmation that "God, beginning and
end of all things, can be known with certainty by the natural
light of reason through the medium of things created" (*Denz.*
S.3004). So, with the prophet Habacuc, we can agree: "He
who is just lives by Faith."

Why, then, is faith so difficult for modern man, Pope Paul
wonders. Is it because of "the technical scientific mentality...happy with its fruitfulness...proud of its inven-
tions...[which] has advanced into the realm of science
fiction where everything seems explainable and everything
possible?" The pope, like his predecessor Pius XII, whom
he quoted in this address, had no doubt that this mentality is
one of the major obstacles to faith.

St. Paul, in his letter to the Romans, had no doubt about
the reason, in his time, for man's infidelity or lack of faith—
sin. He wrote:

> The wrath of God is revealed from Heaven against all
> ungodliness and wickedness of those men who in wicked-
> ness hold back the truth of God, seeing that what may
> be known about God is manifest to them. *For God has
> manifested it to them.* Since the creation of the world
> His invisible attributes are clearly seen, His everlasting
> power also and *Divinity, being understood through
> the things that are made* [Rom. 1:18–20].

It is evident that the fathers of Vatican I repeated this
teaching of St. Paul almost verbatim in the decree *Dei Filius*.
Pope Paul asks, "Why then do so many men, even learned
ones, maintain the contrary?" and he answered, "Because
they do not use their minds in accordance with the authentic
laws of thought in search of truth. We know this is a serious
statement to make, but such is the case."

St. Paul was not so gentle with the infidels of his day:

> And so [he wrote] they are without excuse, seeing that although they knew God they did not glorify Him as God or give thanks, but became vain in their reasonings, and their senseless minds have been darkened. For while professing to be wise, they have become fools, and they have changed the glory of the Incorruptible God for an image made like to corruptible man and to birds and four-footed beasts and creeping things [Rom. 1:20-23].

How absolutely revelant this is to our modern society, to our secular humanists, our ecology nuts, our whale and bald-eagle and seal lovers, our abortion-minded criminal-coddling liberals, who confuse freedom with licence and moral anarchy—"vain in their reasonings . . . their senseless minds . . . darkened"! Indeed they are without excuse, except the excuse afforded by the *mysterium iniquitatis* to which they have succumbed by refusing to accept what God has freely offered.

God has, as we have just seen, given all men, without exception, the ability to know with certainty that he exists. Agnostic or atheistic scientists who deny that fact are bound inexorably, if they wish to remain credible scientists, to a triple faith: belief that there is order in the universe, that we can know that order, and that it is good for us to know that order. And they have to postulate that there is in the material universe a mysterious innate property or power whereby order was and is produced from disorder. Senseless minds darkened, yes indeed!

But God went further than endowing man with the power of reason. As Pope Paul reminded us in that address of June 12, 1968,

> If we speak of Faith as a true and supernatural knowledge of God, coming from His Revelation, then while our ordinary powers of thought are necessary and must be used, they are not enough. They have to be supported by a special help from God Himself, which we call grace.

That extraordinary and free act whereby God enables man to believe in God's revealing himself, which we call grace, is in a mysterious way analogous to the manner in which God chose to share his creative power with his creature. God does not create a new human individual without the prior procreative act of a set of parents. Similarly, he offers the grace of faith freely; *we must accept it freely.* In the words of the *Catholic Encyclopedia,* "Faith is a mutual and free gift that is exchanged between God and the believer." Here, then, is a definition of faith that characterizes it from the subjective point of view, the point of view of the persons who are involved in the act—God and the believer.

This is why the Holy Father said, as we noted earlier, "Faith is the root of our religion." The word "religion" means a relation, a binding relation, between creature and creator. It is a bond, a power, a virtue. We call it the chief or cardinal theological virtue. It is the hinge of the door through which, and only through which, we can approach the transcendent God.

The pope asks frequently how can it be possible for man to make such a stupendous effort as is required to accept this freely offered gift of God, supernatural faith? He asked it in that address of June 12, 1968, from which we have quoted. And he answered with the words of our divine Lord at the Last Supper: "Let not your hearts be troubled. Believe in God and believe also in Me" (Jn. 14:1). "Christ," the pope said, "enables us to believe, with both natural and supernatural Faith . . . listen once again to His voice . . . it is the voice of truth and of salvation." He emphasized this answer in an address a week later, in which he referred to the forthcoming ending of the Year of Faith and made two observations on how to have a live faith:

> The first of these makes us aware that Faith must be for us a personal fact, a conscious act, willed and deep. This subjective element of Faith is most important today; it has always been necessary because it is part and parcel of the authentic act of Faith. . . . Today it is indispensable. Each one has to express in himself his personal Faith with great awareness and great energy.
>
> The second observation reminds us that *Faith has its focal point in Jesus Christ.* It is, we may say, a personal encounter with Him. He is the Master. He is the supreme point of Revelation. He is the center in which are united, and from which radiate, all the religious truths necessary for our salvation. From Him the Church gets her authority. In Him our Faith finds joy and security, finds life.

So here we have another important definition of faith:

Faith is our personal adherence to Jesus Christ. It is, as Pope Paul said (September 27, 1972), "the principle of our salvific union with Christ." Because he is God, our Savior, who came to reveal to us the incomprehensible, ineffable life of love of the trijune God, faith is the theological virtue that generates hope and charity.

On July 3, 1968, Pope Paul urged his audience to recall the words of St. Paul to the Romans: "If you confess with your mouth the Lord Jesus and believe in your heart that God has raised Him up from the dead, you shall be saved" (Rom. 8:35). His Holiness added, *"That is our compass. In this faithless and tormented sea of the present world let us keep steady to this supreme point, Jesus Christ."* And again he quoted the Apostle Paul, "Whom then shall separate us from the love of Christ? Shall tribulation? or distress? or famine? or nakedness? or danger? or persecution? or the sword? . . . *In all these things we overcome because of Him that loved us"* (Rom. 8:37).

We must now turn our attention to another aspect of the vast and inexhaustible question of faith—the objective aspect—and we might well rephrase our question to What is *the* faith?

In the ultimate theological sense, of course, the object of faith is God himself, God revealing. God is the source of that spark of divine life without which supernatural faith is impossible; that spark is called grace, as we have seen. *He is also that which he is revealing—as much as we can comprehend of his divine nature, as well as what he wills for us.* He chose, in his infinite love and wisdom, to complete that revelation of himself and his plan of salvation for us in the person, life, death, resurrection, and teachings of his own divine Son, made man. Therefore in the objective sense, the faith, as well as a relation of acceptance and adherence to a person, the person of the God-man, *is also a body of truths which we must believe.* We have seen that this body of truths of God's revelation was entrusted to the Church by Christ— the *depositum fidei,* as it is called.

The Church is the guardian of this deposit of revealed truths; the guaranteed, infallible interpreter of their meaning; the only authorized teacher of those truths and their implication for us. In the course of the Church's long history, they have been disputed, elucidated, expounded, and defended by countless thousands of theologians and other experts. But we can thank God every day that he did not leave us at the mercy of the *periti*. We have the Church's supreme magisterium to thank, in his name, for providing from the very beginning a summary—authoritative, yet condensed and abbreviated—of the main truths of the faith. Such summary formulas are called "symbols of faith" by the professional theologian, or the "rule of faith." We know them better by the term "creed."

Pope Paul gave a brief account of the development of the credal formulas in his general audience of July 3, 1968. He noted that, from the earliest days of the Church, the candidates for baptism, the Catechumens, had to learn and recite from memory a synthesis of fundamental dogmas of doctrinal teaching—a catechetical method which, he said, probably originated in Rome. There, at the beginning of the third century, it was recorded in the so-called "apostolic tradition" of Hippolytus in the form of an interrogation similar to that still used in the baptismal liturgy. This text was believed to have originated from the apostles and was seen by St. Ambrose to be "what the Roman Catholic Church always safeguards and preserves." According to St. Augustine, "this is the Faith to be held, set down in a few words in the Creed which is given to the new Christians" (*De fide et symb.*, N. 25; Pl. 40, 196). It subsequently became known as the Apostles' Creed. It was taken up by the Council of Nicea and amplified in the form in which it is still recited in the Mass, with only a few modifications (First Council of Constantinople, in 381, and Pope Benedict VII, in 1014). So even in those early days there was little excuse for ignorance of the essential truths of the faith. (Yet at the end of the second century, Tertullian felt constrained to write *"Ne ignorata damnetur!* Let it [the faith] not be condemned out of ignorance!" [Apol. 1].)

As we know, most of the general councils of the Church were called on to restate, defend, and frequently define, solemnly and infallibly, the central doctrines of the faith, nearly always in response to the denial of one or more of the doctrines. The greatest of the dogmatic councils was undoubtedly Trent, which, as we saw, covered many of the basic teachings.

Then there was Vatican I, the centenary of which was commemorated by Pope Paul on the Feast of the Immaculate Conception in 1969. He obviously felt the need to re-emphasize its importance, as he did two days later in addressing a general audience.

> It deserves commemoration [he said] on account of its topicality, the importance which it has for our time . . . its relevance . . . because of its teachings . . . because they are authoritative definitions of a Divine teaching contained in Holy Scripture, or coming down to us from the Apostolic Preaching, by way of Tradition . . . because the First and the Second Vatican Council complement each other.

We know what Pope Paul put into the Second Vatican Council documents by his personal and timely interventions and what high hopes he had that they would serve as comprehensive though not absolutely exhaustive accounts and restatements of the perennial teachings of the Church.

Undoubtedly, when he declared the Year of Faith in 1968, in honor of the centenary of the martyrdom of Saints Peter and Paul, it was the hope and intention that finally, perhaps, some fruits of the Second Vatican Council would begin to be evident in a renewal and increase of faith. And he said so frequently, and in no uncertain words, during that Year of Faith. He concluded it not with an erudite discussion or amplification of the documents of the recent council but with his own credo of the people of God. It is, as he said in referring to it in October 1968,

> a profession of Faith — a repetition, amplified with explicit references to some doctrinal points, of the Nicene Creed, the celebrated formula of Faith drawn up at the First Ecumenical Council. . . .
>
> From being a brief synthesis of the principal truths believed by the Catholic Church, both Latin and Oriental, this Creed has taken on the solemnity of an official act of our Faith. . . . When we recite the Creed we should always keep in mind this combination of objective Faith (the truths believed) with subjective Faith

(the virtuous act of assent to those truths).

Why have we drawn the attention of the Church to these combined elements in the profession of Faith? . . . for two reasons. First, because as the Council of Trent says . . . "Faith is the beginning of human salvation, the foundation and root of all justification" (Sess. VI, c. 8). Secondly, because today, contrary to what should happen with human progress, Faith, or rather adherence to Faith, has become more difficult . . . because of the attacks on the laws of speculative thought . . . the irresponsible spirit of the absurd, the rejection of logic and metaphysics. . . . *Faith is not fideism, that is, belief deprived of rational grounds. It is not merely the subconscious search for some religious experience; it is possession of Truth, it is certainty.*

In the preamble to his credo Pope Paul indicated that what he was about to do was in fulfillment of the mandate entrusted by Christ to Peter, namely, "to confirm our brothers in the Faith." "We have wished," he said, "to offer to the Living God the homage of a profession of Faith . . . to give, on behalf of all the People of God, a firm witness to the Divine Truth entrusted to the Church to be announced to all nations."

It is not possible in this discussion to deal adequately with the credo of the people of God, the credo of Pope Paul VI. It is an immensely rich compendium of the truths of the faith and forms a core program of catechetical instruction that could scarcely be completed in many study sessions. Therefore let us restrict ourselves to a brief comparison of this creed with that of Nicea. The first superficial glance suggests that the most striking thing is not what they have in common but the difference between them. Pope Paul's credo is a good deal longer and seems more wordy and complex in its syntax than the Nicene Creed. Having made this observation, one almost immediately has a *déjà vu*. Did we not have the same feeling about the Nicene profession of faith, in comparison with the spare, simple language and summary form of the Apostles' Creed?

Do we not recall wondering at the profound Christologic proclamation of the Nicene formula—"God of God, Light of Light, True God of True God, begotten, not made, consubstantial with the Father . . . —wondering if it meant the same as the simple phrase in the Apostles' Creed: "and in Jesus Christ, His only Son, Our Lord"?

But it did not take too many years of sound catechetical instruction to realize that the Nicene formula was clearly an expansion, a development, a rendering explicit what was and is implied in the simple statement of belief in Jesus Christ, the *only* Son of God. So as we examine Pope Paul's profession of faith we see that it, too, is characterized by expansion, development, and explication of the deposit of truths contained in the Nicene credal statements. Perhaps one example will make this clear.

Nowhere in the Nicene Creed do we find explicit reference to the angels or the soul. Yet the reality and created nature of angels and the human soul are implied in the Nicene opening and fundamental expression of belief in "God . . . Maker . . . of all things, visible and *invisible*." Pope Paul, in *his* opening credal profession, refers to God as "Creator of things visible . . . *of things invisible such as the pure spirits which are also called angels, and . . . in each man of his spiritual and immortal soul.*" He thus explicitly states belief in what is implicitly contained in the one word "invisible" in the Nicene Creed.

As we study and compare both creeds, we should note a few other points. Both creeds are trinitarian as well as monotheistic. This is much more evident in Pope Paul's credo, which immediately proclaims belief in one only God, Father, Son and Holy Spirit. The trinitarian structure of the Nicene Creed is apparent only after one has read most of it, whereas, of course, it is identical to Pope Paul's credo in its immediate declaration of belief in one God.

Another point to be noted is that Pope Paul's summary of trinitarian doctrine is much more complete and explicit than what is contained in the Nicene Creed. We must recall that the latter was formulated in response to the Arian heresy, which denied the divinity of Christ. So we find that the emphasis in the Nicene Creed is Christological; almost half of it is concerned with establishing and accurately professing the truth about Christ as God-made-man and redeemer, risen from the dead and ascended into heaven.

It is no slur on the fathers of Nicea to say that Pope Paul deals more even-handedly with each of the three divine Persons! It is also evident that he makes several more explicit statements about them than we find in the Nicene Creed. For instance, he emphasizes God's primal revelation of his nature to Moses in the words "I am Who am," and the essence of his revelation, through and in Jesus Christ, that God is love.

In speaking of our blessed Lord, Pope Paul refers not only to those truths pertaining to him as redeemer, such as his death, resurrection, ascension, and his kingship and judgeship, as does the Nicene Creed, but also to his role as teacher. His paragraph on the Holy Spirit simply expands the statements of the Nicene formula, after repeating them, by emphasizing the role of the Holy Spirit as life giver and sanctifier, not only of individual Christians but the entire Church. Similarly, the short statement of belief in the Church, which we find in the Nicene Creed, is expanded into a miniature treatise on authentic ecclesiology—a rather marvelous synthesis of all the truths about the Church that we can find in the decrees and documents of both Vatican councils.

These ecclesiologic statements of Pope Paul are noteworthy for several truths not contained in the Nicene Creed, save by implication:

1. The role of Mary, Mother of God and Mother of the Church.

2. The foundation of the Church on Peter, its nature as a hierarchical, visible society, and at the same time a spiritual community; its necessary role in the salvation both of its known members and those who are invincibly ignorant of it but who believe in God and seek to do his will according to their own lights; the teaching authority of the Church and her infallible magisterium; her role in temporal affairs, which stems from her supernatural and spiritual mission and is always illuminated by and subordinated to it.

3. The sacramental aspects of the Church: baptism, penance and reconciliation, and above all, the Mass and the eucharistic real presence of our Lord. In this latter

section we find a condensed but powerful restatement of the Mass as sacrifice, the doctrine of transubstantiation, and the real presence in the Blessed Sacrament—"the Living Heart of each of our Churches," as Pope Paul said.

We find, of course, other striking and consoling reaffirmations of traditional orthodox Catholic beliefs in Pope Paul's credo, such as *the perpetual virginity of Mary* ("She remained ever a Virgin," he said), *the fact and the consequences of original sin* (surely a necessary restatement of belief in the face of the new Pelagians who infest the Church), *the existence of hell and purgatory*, the necessity of infant baptism, and so on.

We have by no means exhausted the richness of this precious compendium of the true faith given us by our Holy Father. And no wonder it was received with so much disdain by the new-breed catechists. We can only pray that the Lord will enlighten them in his own good time.

But let us not be smug and complacent in our joyful acceptance of this credo of the people of God, with which Pope Paul brought the Year of Faith to a close, and which, better than any other documentation, shows him as the man of faith that he is. Let us realize and continually remind ourselves, as he does so often in his addresses, that faith is a free gift of God, and that our acceptance of this gift does not guarantee that we have the fullness of the faith, nor excuse us from striving to increase it. Let us say with the centurion and with Pope Paul, "Lord, I believe, do You help my unbelief" (Mk. 9:24), and let us continue with the pope:

> Let my Faith be *full and unreserved* . . .
> Let my Faith be *free* . . .
> Let my Faith be *certain* . . .
> Let my Faith be *strong* . . .
> Let my Faith be *joyful* . . .
> Let my Faith be *industrious* . . .
> Lord, let my Faith be *humble* and not presume to be based on the experience of my thought and of my feeling; but let it surrender to the testimony of the Holy Spirit, and not have any better guarantee than in docility to Tradition and to the Authority of the Magisterium of the Holy Church, Amen [address of October 30, 1968].

8. What Church Did Jesus Christ Actually Found?

This is surely the most outlandish question we have asked ourselves so far in our reflections on the teachings of our Holy Father, Pope Paul VI. He has asked some strange questions, however, as we have seen, and has provided his own unique answers, in full conformity with the faith handed down to him (and to us through him) but expressed according to his mind and will, as is fitting. He asked the question that is the title for this chapter on August 29, 1973, in an address in which he spoke of his hope for reconciliation during the approaching Holy Year.

He adverted to the rather disconcerting and unprecedented fact that dissenters from authentic magisterial teaching "would like to legalize, by claiming the widest tolerance, their own official membership in the Church and annul any hypothesis of schism or self-excommunication." He spoke of the lack of charity that characterized this bitter and joyless negative spirit of contestation, and he recalled St. Paul's hymn to charity: "Love is patient and kind, love is not jealous or boastful; it is not arrogant or rude. Love does not insist on its own way; it is not irritable or resentful; it does not rejoice at wrong but rejoices in the right. Love bears all things, believes all things, hopes all things, endures all things" (1 Cor. 13:4–7).

He went on to speak of the second characteristic of this contestation and dissent, this "division so much felt in the Catholic Church today . . . in the minds, in the ideas, in the attitude of many who still, and often with a stubborn sense of their own superiority, call themselves Catholics, but after their own fashion." This second characteristic is the facile and illogical and unlawful distinction they seek to make "between the institutional and the charismatic Church; between the Church of Jesus Christ and that of the people guided by the Holy Spirit; between the One, Holy, Catholic and Apostolic Church and a church conceived according to one's own personal views or even according to one's own subjective spiritual tastes."

He identified two chief negative consequences, "*disobedience, and pluralism beyond its legitimate limits*," and he categorically denied the substantial distinction between the institutional Church and the presumed purely charismatic Church.

"*What Church did Jesus actually found?*" he asked, and—answered: "*Jesus founded His Church upon Peter, upon the Apostles; He founded no other churches. There are not several churches; complete and perfect in conception, there exists One only.* And this is the Church to which Jesus has sent the Holy Spirit, in order that the institutional Church may live through the animation of the Holy Spirit."

We have, therefore, a categorical answer to our question and we will explore the necessary elaborations of this straightforward and unambiguous statement of fact, which is absolutely and irrevocably opposed to the liberal Protestant view, no less than to the Modernist opinion within the Church. The former is best summed up in the writings of Adolf Harnack, professor of theology in the University of Berlin around the beginning of this century. The latter was perhaps expounded best by a French priest, Alfred Loisy, a contemporary of Harnack.

Harnack's thesis was that the texts of the New Testament (which he defended vigorously and effectively as historical documents) prove that the entire burden of Christ's teaching could be summed up in the twin truths of the fatherhood of God and the kingdom of heaven, namely, the spiritual dominion of God our Father in our souls. The idea of a church, except in that invisible and entirely spiritual sense, was entirely foreign to the mind of Christ, according to Harnack. How, then, did he explain the emergence of a church? The pressure of persecution, first by the Jews, then by the Romans, was the first reason for the Christians to organize themselves.

Then came the attacks from within: the early heresies, especially the Gnostics, which forced the primitive Christian communities to formulate their beliefs in a variety of credal formulas. And so formalism of doctrine emerged, together with formality of structure, until a fully regimented ecclesiastical society emerged.

Harnack even provided dates for this evolution of the Church—the time of Clement of Alexandria and Tertullian being a sort of watershed. Before them, something was still left of the liberty of Christ; after them, it was lost. In the East, the civil power in the Byzantine Empire overwhelmed and absorbed the Church. In the West, the opposite happened: the Church became the empire. Canon law was simply Roman law applied to church affairs; the Roman pontiff became the counterpart of the old Roman *pontifex maximus*—one could even equate Peter and Paul with Romulus and Remus. Harnack certainly had no quarrel with Thomas Hobbes when he wrote, "What is the Papacy but the ghost of the deceased Roman Empire sitting on the ruins thereof?"

Loisy arrived at a somewhat similar conclusion, namely, that the Church had evolved under the pressure of events. According to Loisy, the essential teaching of Christ was the proximity of the kingdom of God. Christ, in this view, was as ignorant as the modern-day eschatologists in the theologically rarefied air of California and other Western states. He believed and taught, according to Loisy, that the end of the world was close at hand, but when, after his death, it became evident that this was not so, the apostles and disciples whom he had left began to think of organizing a permanent society with rules and conditions of membership.

It is abundantly clear that the liberal Protestant theology, exemplified by Harnack, and the Modernist theology, as put forth by Loisy and a whole school of pseudo theologians since his day, have simply revived the old Arian heresy and dressed it up in some new clothes. In effect, they deny the divinity of Christ. But it will not hold water, any more than it did in the fourth century.

Christ was, and is, fully human and fully divine. He knew exactly why he had come into human history and the will of God the Father for mankind. He told Simon Peter exactly what he intended when he said to him—we all know the text so well—"You are Peter, and upon this rock I will build my Church, and the gates of hell will not prevail against it." No amount of semantic gymnastics or verbal sleight of hand can get around that forthright statement.

Of course liberal exegetes, such as Harnack, and liberal Protestants such as our Modernist historical relativists, point to other statements of the Lord, suggesting that he had in mind a spiritual community, not a visible church. They recall John's gospel, in which we find statements such as "The Kingdom of God is within you" and "The hour cometh and now is at hand when the true adorers shall adore the Father in spirit and in truth."

But of course these texts *do* mean what they say. The Church, the kingdom of God, *is* a spiritual communion, an invisible bond linking men with God and with one another. Faith *is*, as St. Paul says, "the argument of things that appear not." But it would be just as illogical to argue that, because there is a spiritual, an invisible aspect to the Church, a soul, as we have always been taught, therefore there is no body, no visible society called the Church, attributable to Christ, as to conclude that our Lord himself was invisible while on earth because his Godhead was an object of faith and was not visible.

Pope Paul has frequently and categorically denied such an absurd proposition. Thus on January 19, 1970, addressing participants at the International Congress of Canon Law, he said:

> You have recognized that the Church founded by Christ is a visible society. The idea that the Church may be invisible is revealed as being utopian, not to say simply self-contradictory. That was asserted by scholars and movements which in other times adopted a purely spiritualist and liberal interpretation of Christianity. Likewise the tendency spread to some degree today among persons and Christian groups to claim a charismatic voice of their own . . . in order to emancipate one's own conscience and conduct and that of others from the Church's normative power.

The Church was founded by Christ on Peter, but also on

the other apostles together with him. The post-resurrection accounts of our Lord's instructions to them, the documentation in the Acts of the Apostles on the fulfillment of Christ's promises to send the Holy Spirit, in which the Church began its earthly career, including the marvelous story of the First Council—all these put the question beyond all doubt. And beyond all doubt our Lord virtually identified himself with the apostles: "He that heareth you heareth Me."

Pope Paul echoed this truth when he spoke, very emotionally, to the Assembly of Asian Bishops in Manila on November 28, 1970, on the occasion of his journey to Asia and Oceania.

> Christ is here [he said], He is here through the reality, ever repeated — a gathering in His name. He is here through the Faith that makes Him live in each one of us. *He is here also through the coming of Our Humble Person,* to whom, as a lowly Successor of Peter, is applied in a very special way the title, Vicar of Christ. *And Christ Our Lord is here through the apostolic ministry entrusted to each of us,* and through the collegial relationship that joins us together. We, the successors of the Apostles and the pastors of the Church of God, are invested with the power not only of representing Christ, but also of making present on earth and in time His voice and His saving action. Christ is here. . . . All of us meeting here are successors of the Apostles. We have received from Christ Himself the mandate, the power, His Spirit, to carry on and spread His mission. We are the heirs of the Apostles; we are Christ working in history and the world; we are the ministers of His pastoral government of the Church; *we are the institutional organ, entrusted with dispensing the mysteries of God.* . . . This seems to us a suitable occasion for restating our firm support of the doctrine of the apostolic nature of the Church. We must realize that this doctrine establishes the permanence and the authenticity of the foundation of the Church by Christ; *it marks the boundaries of ecclesial communion.*

Earlier that year, Pope Paul had made similar statements on the apostolic and hierarchical nature of the Church founded by Christ. On April 15, 1970, in the course of a general audience, he spoke of two essential features of the design which derives from Christ and is concerned with announcing his gospel of salvation: *jealous textual fidelity to the message, and the distinctive and characteristic office conferred on the apostolic succession to guard the message, propagate it, defend it, and teach it.* "This shows," he said, "that the Church possesses within herself an organ which instructs her and guarantees the genuine expression of God's word. *It is the Hierarchical Magisterium, and it generates the Christian people.*" And he recalled St. Paul's claim to this same generative and vivifying teaching function in writing to the Corinthians: "For you may have ten thousand instructors in regard to Christ, but you have not many fathers; I begot you in Christ Jesus through the Gospel" (1 Cor. 4:15).

And so, said the pope, "between Christ and Christians stands a teaching power, the Hierarchical Magisterium."

This go-between was excluded, he said, by the Protestant Reformation, which claimed to "put every follower of Christ into direct contact with 'Scripture alone,' " with the sad result of separating non-Catholic Christians into innumerable factions and sects.

> What has become of the unity of faith that should make Christians brothers? We might also ask, if Sacred Scripture were enough to generate Christianity, where does Sacred Scripture come from, if not from an oral Apostolic Magisterium, which preceded it, which produced it, which guaranteed it, and which preserved it? It is necessary to note that *Christ did not found an abstract religion, a mere school of religious thought. He set up a community of Apostles, of teachers with the task of spreading His Message and so giving rise to a society of believers: His Church.* He promised the spirit of truth to His Church and then sent it. He gave it an assurance that no hostile power would be able to prevail over it.

The Holy Father refuted the twin arguments put forward by dissenters seeking emancipation from the ecclesiastical magisterium, namely, liberty of science and freedom of conscience, and he concluded by quoting St. Augustine's statement, "I would not believe the Gospel, were I not moved to do so by the Church's authority."

The Church, of course, is more than a teaching authority; she is not only the teacher of faith but is the object of faith. We say in the Creed at Mass, "I believe in One, Holy, Catholic and Apostolic Church." Furthermore, she is composed of members other than those with apostolic pastoral authority. There is, after all, a society of believers resulting from apostolic pastoral activity, a Christian people generated by the apostolic hierarchical magisterium, as the pope said; a people of which the magisterium is part, a people known especially since the Second Vatican Council as the people of God.

It is of great significance that so much attention has been paid in modern times by the Church to her own mystery. As Pope Paul said in an address on September 5, 1973, "Everyone knows that doctrinal study of the Church is comparatively recent; there is no real treatment of the subject in St. Thomas' *Summa*. It was necessary to wait until the crisis of the Reformation to have a systematic and organic exposition of the Church." The Holy Father referred to the famous one by St. Robert Bellarmine, *De Militanti Ecclesia*, and to Pope Pius XII's masterly synthesis in the encyclical *Mystici Corporis*, issued in 1943, at what must have seemed an incongruous time to the men of this world, who were involved in mutual killing and destruction. "Nero fiddling while Rome was burning" might well have been the comment of Hobbes, if he were alive.

Was it not, however, yet one more example of prophetic witness by the supreme magisterium, analogous in a real way with the astounding and uncompromising declaration in *Lumen Gentium* at a time when the cold war still preoccupied the governments and people of most nations?

The council fathers said, "It has pleased God to make men holy and save them not merely as individuals without any mutual bonds, but by making them into a single people, a people which acknowledges Him in truth and serves Him in holiness" (*L.G.*, 9). Astounding, I say—unbelievable naiveté and hopeless utopianism, in the opinion of many.

Yet is it not what the Church has always done, especially in times of crisis, namely, to reiterate the gospel of the Lord, to hold up for all men to see, if they will, the divine plan of salvation? How can we not see, therefore, the providential reasons for the emergence of this splendid constitution on the Church as one of the main fruits of the Second Vatican Council? We have alluded to it as a most timely and appropriate vision of the Church, which will stand the members of Christ's mystical body in good stead in all the trials to come.

The issuance of this document did not still the voices of

dissent—clamorous, quasi expert, numerous—any more than Pope Pius XII's encyclical *Mystici Corporis* did in his day. And so, on June 24, 1973, the Sacred Congregation for the Doctrine of the Faith issued a declaration, ratified and confirmed by Pope Paul VI, a document of great importance and value, known, as is customary, by its opening Latin words, *Mysterium Ecclesiae.* It is given, in the English version, a revealing title: *Declaration in Defense of the Catholic Doctrine on the Church against Certain Errors of the Present Day.*

It is of importance and value because it is authoritative. It is brief and understandable and to the point, neither wasting nor mincing words. And it provides an excellent summary of the main truths about the Church defined at Vatican I and reaffirmed by Vatican II. It deserves, therefore, our closest attention so that we make it our very own. It summarizes the mind of our Holy Father, Pope Paul VI, on the answers to our question. He alone can safely say, "We have the mind of Christ."

A short introduction sets forth, clearly and simply, the reason for such a declaration at this time. It draws attention to the numerous writings of theologians on the mystery of the Church, "on which the Second Vatican Council shed fresh light," and to the fact that while some of these studies were helpful, others, "through the use of ambiguous or even erroneous language, have obscured Catholic doctrine, and at times have gone so far as to be opposed to Catholic Faith even in fundamental matters."

It also adverts to the remedial efforts of the bishops of several countries and those of the second General Synod of Bishops, and states the purpose of this document: "To gather together a number of truths concerning the mystery of the Church which at the present time are being either denied or endangered." It added the significant intention of following "above all the lines laid down by the two Vatican Councils."

Then, immediately, the declaration affirms the unity or oneness of Christ's Church, which "after His Resurrection Our Savior handed over to Peter as Shepherd, commissioning him and the other Apostles to propagate and govern her, and which He erected for all ages as the pillar and mainstay of the truth."

What a condensed and pregnant statement that is! Note that it affirms not only that the Church is one but that she is hierarchical and apostolic and permanent, and universal or catholic, under one head, Peter, assisted by the other apostles, and that her primary purpose "for all ages" is to bear witness to and maintain intact the truth—the revealed truth of God, the deposit of faith.

It reaffirms the fundamental statement of *Lumen Gentium*, that *this Church of Christ is constituted and organized as a visible society, and subsists in the Catholic Church, which is identified as that Church which is governed by the pope, the successor of Peter, and the bishops in union with him.* Further, it asserts with *Lumen Gentium* that "*it is through Christ's Catholic Church alone, which is the general means of salvation, that the fullness of the means of salvation can be obtained.*" And the same Catholic Church "*has been endowed with all divinely revealed truth and with all the means of grace.*"

Then it explains, in a few pithy and cogent sentences, how the Church is holy yet always needs purification—*ecclesia semper reformanda.* It provides the only basis for a sound ecumenical movement and esteem for our separated brethren, and reminds Catholics they are bound to profess that they belong to that Church which Christ founded, which is governed by the successors of Peter and the other apostles. They are "the depositaries of the original Apostolic tradition, living and intact, which is the permanent heritage of doctrine and holiness of that same Church."

This section ends with implicit condemnation of several principal tenets of the process theologians:

> The followers of Christ are therefore not permitted to imagine that Christ's Church is nothing more than a collection, divided but still possessing a certain unity, of churches and ecclesial communities. Nor are they free to hold that Christ's Church nowhere really exists today and that it is to be considered only as an end which all churches and ecclesial communities must strive to reach.

The rest of the document reaffirms the infallibility of (1) the universal Church, an infallibility of belief, based, as *Lumen Gentium* said, on a supernatural instinct of faith, and (2) the Church's magisterium, an infallibility of teaching. It quotes the relevant text from the decrees of *both* Vatican councils. It also points out the proper role of all the members of the Church in this infallible preservation of those truths that are to be believed with divine faith, conceding that the faithful contribute to the understanding and development of doctrine, *but asserting that however much the supreme magisterium avails itself of the insights of the faithful, its office is not reduced to ratifying the assent expressed by the faithful.*

Several other Modernist errors are condemned, e.g., that the Church has taught error in some propositions that the magisterium has promulgated to be held irrevocably; that dogmatic formulas that are derived from other principal dogmas need not be held to be *de fide divina* (believed with divine faith); that dogmatic formulas (or some category of them) cannot signify truth in a determinate way but are only approximations and can and must be radically restated (i.e., it condemns dogmatic relativism).

There is a very clear, succinct section on the distinction between the common priesthood of the laity and the ministerial or hierarchical priesthood, the nature and functions of both, and the limitations on the former.

The entire document is of immense importance, but it is in the very first section that we find expressed so clearly, once more, the fundamental answers to our question, What Church did Jesus Christ actually found? *He founded his Church on Peter and the other apostles, and that church is the Catholic Church.*

> They were a strange lot, these eleven. They would be succeeded by men stranger than themselves. He who had foreseen Peter's denial . . . foresaw whole hierarchies moving into heresy or cowering before rulers. . . . *He foresaw you and me!* Yet this was His choice: the gifts of truth and life should come through these men and their successors: in union with them we are in union with Him, all days until the end of the world. [F. J. Sheed, *To Know Christ Jesus* (New York: Sheed and Ward, 1962), p. 362]

9. The Pope and the Mother of God

It is necessary to recall one of the important documents of Vatican II and the deliberations about it if we are to understand the breadth and the depth of Pope Paul's teachings on the Blessed Virgin Mary. That document is the dogmatic constitution on the Church, *Lumen Gentium.*

When Pope John XXIII conceived the idea of convoking a general council to complete the work begun by the First Vatican Council, it was to be expected that the major focus of the council would be on the Church herself.

He spoke of *aggiornamento,* a much abused and much misunderstood word, and hope sprang up anew in Modernist ecclesiastical breasts. He spoke of throwing open the windows of the Church, and in the words of one old pastor, for a start, nothing emerged but "hot air"!

There were those who recalled the prophecy made by St. John Bosco in August 1862, concerning an ecumenical council in the next century which would be followed by chaos in the Church.

But as the council progressed and approved documents began to emerge after Pope Paul's many decisive interventions, one was reassured that indeed the Holy Spirit was working through the council and that all would be well.

Nevertheless, as happened after Trent, the dissidents swiftly set to work misinterpreting the council documents, and in the name of the council and in the interest of "ecumenism," a word as abused as *aggiornamento*, these modern-day iconoclasts sought to demolish traditional beliefs and devotions. The council, they claimed, had changed everything. The council had downgraded the position of the Mother of God. The rosary was just so much superstitious mumbo-jumbo, they cried. In some cases, avant-garde priests and religious plucked the rosary beads from the hands of the pious faithful and broke them.

What a lie they spread, and what a tribute to the resurgent power of Satan!

You must know by now that the Second Vatican Council, far from downgrading and belittling the traditional and orthodox beliefs and devotional practices related to the Mother of God, placed them on a firmer and better-developed theological and doctrinal foundation.

The council fathers, you will recall, devoted chapter 8 of the fundamental and profound dogmatic constitution on the Church to "the role of the Blessed Virgin Mary, Mother of God, in the mystery of Christ and the Church." In this chapter all the age-old teaching of the Church about Mary is reaffirmed and all sons of the Church are admonished "that the Cult, especially the Liturgical Cult of the Blessed Virgin, be fostered . . . that practices and exercises of devotion toward her be treasured as recommended by the teaching authority of the Church in the course of centuries."

The council came very close to calling Mary "Mother of the Church" in chapter 8, and Pope Paul made this conciliar suggestion explicit in the speech he gave at the closing of the third session of Vatican II, at which *Lumen Gentium* was ratified and promulgated. He recalled that the council's work had been entrusted to Mary and Joseph by Pope John right from the start and that he, Pope Paul, regarded her as the protectress of the council: "the witness of our toil, our most kindly adviser."

He was overjoyed with the fact that, as he saw it, the

crown and summit of the dogmatic constitution on the Church was the chapter dedicated to our Lady.

> It is the first time, in fact, and saying it fills our souls with profound emotion, that an Ecumenical Council presents such a vast synthesis of the Catholic doctrine regarding the place which the Blessed Mary occupies in the mystery of Christ and of the Church . . . of which . . . she is the greatest, finest, principal, most elect part.

He pinpointed the theological basis for this unique position of Mary as the mystic union of the Church with Christ, the primary source of the sanctifying effectiveness of the Church, a union which, he said, *"We cannot conceive as separate from her who is the Mother of the Word Incarnate and whom Jesus Christ Himself wanted closely united to Himself for our Salvation."*

> Meditation on these close relationships between Mary and the Church, so clearly established in today's conciliar constitution, makes us feel that this is the most solemn and appropriate moment to fulfill a wish which . . . very many Council fathers made their own. . . . *Therefore, for the glory of the Virgin Mary and for our own consolation we proclaim the Most Blessed Mary Mother of the Church, that is to say of all the people of God, of the faithful as well as the pastors.*

It is difficult to be convinced of the intelligence of the non-Catholic commentator on *Lumen Gentium* in the Abbott edition of the Vatican II documents. This commentator, Albert C. Outler, referred to the "studied ambiguities" of chapter 8, the chapter on our Lady, in his closing paragraphs, whereas referring to it earlier he had said it "may well have the effect, among other things, of recalling Protestants to an important aspect of Christian faith that they have tended to underestimate, in their reaction to what was deemed the excesses of conventional mariology."

Can he have read chapter 8 with any understanding and insight? He surely cannot have listened to Pope Paul's closing speech at the third council session, or if he did, the meaning and force of the pope's solemn proclamation of the most blessed Mary as Mother of the Church eluded him.

Outler had one insight, however: *Lumen Gentium* was the major contribution of the council and the major task ahead was to decipher its *real* meaning and translate it into action. We can accept that, but we must insist that the authentic interpreter of the meaning of the council is Pope Paul, whether acting personally or collegially.

So let us hear him on May 29, 1968, when he spoke to his general audience on the teaching of the Second Vatican Council on our Blessed Mother:

> We must not let this period [the month of May] end without reviving our devotion to Our Lady, Virgin Mother of Christ and our spiritual mother too . . . *the most beautiful flower of human nature redeemed by Christ.*
>
> This we must do in accordance with the spirit of the Council . . . the Council had no wish to expound new doctrines about her, just as it did not aim to say everything possible about her; but it did present Mary most holy in such a way and with such titles that everyone . . . must not only feel strengthened . . . but must also feel drawn to model his devotion in accordance with the broad, authentic, enchanting vision which the magnificent and meaningful conciliar pages offer.

He asked "What are these visions?" and said he found it hard to answer; he suggested his audience reread and meditate on chapter 8 of *Lumen Gentium*. But then, characteristically, he pointed out the essential basic summary notions: Mary presented not in solitary splendor, as it were, but defined as a unique being precisely by reason of the divine and mysterious relationships which encompass her. *She is presented in a divine trinitarian setting so that, in contemplating her, we cannot but see and adore the blessed Trinity.* Yet she was a daughter of the race of Adam, our own race, and it is because of this that we are able to approach her. This also explains, he felt, the priority in practice which devotion to Mary often assumes in the religious life of many devout souls.

But Mary herself will not let us stop there. It is she herself, Pope Paul explained, "who then draws us along with her in her transcendent flight toward God." "*Remember the Magnificat,*" he exclaimed, and added, "*Our Lady belongs wholly to Christ—through Him, with Him, in Him.*" These words, the concluding doxology of every approved eucharistic prayer in the Mass, apply to his Mother in a very special way. As Pope Paul said,

> Just as we cannot form an idea of Christ without refer-
> ence to the supreme truths of the Gospel regarding His
> Incarnation and Redemption, so we cannot leave out of
> consideration the presence of Mary and the ministrations
> which she was called on to fulfill in the actual realization
> of these same truths." No one has come nearer to Christ
> . . . so closely united to Him . . . so loved by Him. . . .
> No one has had so great a faith in Christ . . . so great a
> trust in His goodness. . . . No one . . . had so great a love
> for Christ . . . not only because she was His Mother, but
> because in her the Holy Spirit was the vivifying and lov-
> ing principle of her Divine maternity. It was this charity
> of the Holy Spirit that associated her with her Son's Pas-
> sion; and at Pentecost when the Holy Spirit came upon
> the Apostles and herself, this charity overflowed in her
> and made her the spiritual mother of the new-born Church
> and indeed of the Church throughout the centuries. St.
> Bernard stated this very well when he wrote, "Coming to
> her the Holy Spirit filled her with grace for herself; when
> the same Spirit pervaded her again she became super-
> abundant and redounding in grace for us also."

It is because of this, Pope Paul said, that she could and should be called the Mother of the Church. This is what the council saw in Mary, he assured us, and it is clearly a vision he made his own.

It is both easy and difficult to put together an anthology of Pope Paul's teachings and utterances about our blessed Lady—easy because of the wealth of published material available, difficult because of the breadth and depth of his faith and his reflections on the unique place of Mary in the divine economy.

Within a few months of the approval and official promulgation of the dogmatic constitution on the Church and Pope Paul's solemn proclamation of our Lady as Mother of the Church, the pope issued his second encyclical. The first was *Ecclesiam Suam*, which we discussed earlier; this second encyclical was an appeal to the bishops of the whole world and to us, through them, for prayers to the Blessed Mother for her continued help with the Second Vatican Council and for peace. The pope recalled the custom, dear to his predecessors, of choosing this month, dedicated to Mary, for inviting the people to offer up public prayers for the needs of the

Church and to avert impending dangers from the world. So, he said, he felt the need to send out a similar appeal.

He drew attention briefly to the significance of the council, what had been accomplished so far and what remained to be done, and declared, "To obtain God's light and blessings on this great volume of work ahead of us, we place our confidence in her whom we had the joy of proclaiming Mother of the Church at the last session. *From the beginning of the Council she has been unstinting in her loving help*, and will certainly not fail to continue her assistance to the final stage of the work."

He went on to speak of the dangers to world peace on the international level, as well as the various local wars, massacres, and terrorism.

"But peace," he said, "comes from Heaven, a gift from God. And it can only be obtained by prayer, especially prayer to the Virgin Mary, who is the Queen of Peace."

For though we know that men's sins weigh heavy in the scales of God's justice and provoke just punishment, "We also know that the Lord is 'The Father of Mercies and the God of all Comfort,' and that *Mary Most Holy is His appointed steward and the generous bestower of the treasures of His mercy*." So he prayed that she might prevail on God, lord of the winds and storms, to still the tempest in men's hearts; and he urged the bishops to make provision for special prayers in every diocese and every parish during the month of May, *solemn public prayers*, and *especially the rosary*, "so dear to Our Lady and so highly recommended by the Supreme Pontiffs."

In the following year, 1966, he issued another urgent appeal in the encyclical *Christi Matris Rosarii*, an appeal for peace and prayers for peace, to him who is the Prince of Peace, but also to her who, as St. Irenaeus said, "was made the cause of salvation for the whole human race." He referred again to the titles and prerogatives that justify our confidence in the Blessed Mother and again stressed the importance of the rosary, "this prayer . . . well-suited to God's people, acceptable to the Mother of God and powerful in obtaining gifts from Heaven." He begged the bishops "to give a lead and urge by exhortation . . . the devout recitation of the Rosary during the month of October."

In May 1967, Pope Paul gave the most striking public witness to his faith and his trust in the Blessed Mother: he made a pilgrimage to Fatima. He summed up the fundamental motives for this pilgrimage in a brief speech he made to the president of Portugal when he landed on Portuguese soil.

> We, too, come as a pilgrim. It is our ardent desire to offer a filial homage to the sublime Mother of God in the Cova da Iria. We will now go there in a spirit of prayer and penance to beseech Our Lady of Fatima that she may bring about the reign of the inestimable blessing of peace in the Church and in the world.

Peace in the Church and in the world! How often has this anguished prayer been wrung from the heart and soul of this suffering pope as he contemplated the havoc being wrought in the Church and in the world by Satan and his minions! The power and the fury that characterize these devastating attacks are surely evidence enough for all but the willfully blind of the truth of those prophecies of Our Lady of Fatima— those prophecies that clearly told us what would come upon us if we do not heed her warnings—those prophecies that re-echo the grave and terrible words of her Son: *"Repent and do penance, or you shall all likewise perish."*

In his sermon at the Mass he celebrated at Fatima, the Holy Father again stated the reasons for his visit: to honor the holy Virgin Mary, his faith in her divine Son, to celebrate the fiftieth anniversary of the apparitions and the twenty-fifth anniversary of the consecration of the world to the Immaculate Heart of Mary. He recalled, too, the special intentions for which he was praying: first, for the Church, for its internal peace, and, second, for peace in the world.

"The Ecumenical Council," he asserted, "has revitalized the heart of the Church."

> What terrible damage could be provoked by arbitrary interpretations, not authorized by the teaching of the Church, disrupting its traditional and constitutional structure, replacing the theology of the true and great Fathers of the Church with new and peculiar ideologies, interpretations intent upon stripping the norms of faith of that which modern thought, often lacking rational judgment,

does not understand and does not like. Such interpreta-
tions change the apostolic fervor of redeeming charity to
the negative structures of a profane mentality and of mundane customs. *What a delusion our efforts to arrive at
universal unity would suffer, if we fail to offer to our
Christian brethren, at this moment divided from us, and
to the rest of humanity which lacks our faith in its clear-
cut authenticity and in its original beauty, the patrimony
of truth and of charity of which the Church is the guardian and the dispenser. We want to ask of Mary a living
Church, a holy Church.*

Then he said: "The second intention of our pilgrimage
fills our hearts—the world, peace in the world." Despite all
its enormous material, scientific, and technological progress,
the Holy Father asserted, "you can easily see that the world
is not happy. . . . Two conditions render difficult this his-
toric situation of mankind. It is full of tremendous deadly
armament, and it has not morally progressed as much as it
has scientifically and technically. . . . *Therefore, we say, the
world is in danger.*" No one can disagree with these sobering
words of Pope Paul.

Let us hear the solution he proposed:

> *For this reason we have come to the feet of the Queen
> of Peace to ask her for the gift which only God can give,
> of peace. . . .* Behold, my brothers and children who listen
> to us here, behold the immense and dramatic picture
> which the world and its destinies present to us. It is the
> picture which Our Lady opens up before us, the picture
> which we contemplate with frightened eyes, but ever
> trusting knowledge, *the picture to which we ever draw
> near and to which we pledge ourselves, following the coun-
> sel which Our Lady gave us and which God desires, that
> of prayer and of penance.*

On the same day that Pope Paul gave this unprecedented
public witness at Fatima (May 13, 1967), he had promulgated
in Rome an apostolic exhortation on the Blessed Virgin Mary
titled *Signum Magnum,* "The Great Sign." This "great sign"
was that which the Apostle John saw, "a woman clothed with
the sun, and with the moon at her feet, and on her head a
crown of twelve stars."

This apostolic exhortation is a wonderfully brief and concise summary of the essentials of Mariology as enshrined in
Scripture and tradition and expounded by the fathers of the

Church, the great spiritual writers, and the magisterial teaching of the Holy See. In it, however, the pope stressed two truths:

> Mary is the Mother of the Church not only because she is the Mother of Christ and His most intimate associate . . . but also because "she shines forth to the whole community of the elect as a model of the virtues" (*L.G.*, no. 65). . . . This is a most consoling truth, which, by the free consent of God the All-Wise, is an integrating part of the mystery of human salvation; *therefore it must be held as faith by all Christians.*

This declaration of the pope clarifies the theological note that pertains to this statement, that Mary is the Mother of the Church, namely, that it is a teaching pertaining to the faith, therefore theologically certain.

A little later the pope referred to the perpetual virginity of Mary, which he says "the Church has always believed and professed"—from the fifth general council (the Second Council of Constantinople) in 553, when she was given the title Perpetual Virgin, down to and including the Second Vatican Council (*L.G.*, Acta Apost. Sed. 57, 1965, pp. 58–64). Neither of these truths, therefore, would seem to need definition, yet the temerarious opinions and speculations of lightweight theologians and Scripture experts continue to plague and vex the faith of the people. So we should pray that a solemn definition of both truths will be made in due course, either by the pope alone or with a general council.

The second truth stressed by Pope Paul in *Signum Magnum* flows from the first:

> It is the duty of all Christians to imitate in a reverent spirit the examples of goodness left to them by their heavenly Mother. . . . Imitation of Jesus Christ is undoubtedly the regal way to be followed to attain sanctity and reproduce in ourselves, according to our capacity, the absolute perfection of the heavenly Father; but while the Catholic Church has always proclaimed a truth so sacrosanct, it has also affirmed that imitation of the Virgin Mary, far from distracting souls from the faithful following of Christ, makes it more easy and pleasant for them. . . . *The general norm "Through Mary to Jesus" is therefore valid.*

On October 17, 1971, the Holy Father presided over the

solemn rite of beatification of Father Maximilian Kolbe. In his homily, having reviewed the essential biographical details of the new blessed, the pope declared, "It is impossible to separate the name, the activity and the mission of Blessed Kolbe from that of Mary Immaculate." He referred to a certain mistrust of such a Marian exultation, a mistrust seemingly based on the grounds that two other theological and spiritual movements, the Christological and the ecclesiological movements, were "in competition" with the Mariological one.

> *There is no competition* [the pope asserted]. *Christ, in Kolbe's thought, holds not only the first place, but the only place necessary and sufficient, absolutely speaking, in the economy of salvation*; nor is love of the Church and of her mission forgotten in the doctrinal conception or the apostolic aim of the new blessed. *On the contrary*, it is precisely from her subordinated complementariness, with regard to Christ's cosmological, anthropological and soteriological plan, that the Blessed Virgin derives her every prerogative and greatness. Well we know it. *And Kolbe, like the whole of Catholic doctrine, liturgy and spirituality, sees Mary inserted in the Divine plan, as the "Fixed Term of Eternal Counsel,"* the Fullness of Grace, the Seat of Wisdom, the predestined Mother of Christ, the Queen of the Messianic Kingdom, and at the same time, the Lord's handmaid, the one chosen to offer the Incarnation of the Word her irreplaceable cooperation, as the Mother of the God-man, our Savior. In the words of Louis Bouyer, "Mary is the One through whom men reach Jesus and the One through whom Jesus reaches men" (Bouyer, *La Trane de la Sagesse,* p. 69).

It was no surprise, then, that when Pope Paul decided to promulgate the Holy Year and dedicated it to the twin goals of renewal and reconciliation, he instinctively turned to the Blessed Mother for help. In a general audience address on May 30, 1973, he asked, "What can be the help that enables us to dare, to hope for the aims of the Holy Year? Who can obtain for us the marvelous result which, following the logical demands of the Council, we have proposed?

"The Blessed Virgin, beloved sons! Holy Mary, the Mother of Christ the Savior, the Mother of the Church, our humble and glorious Queen."

In view of the foregoing, it was most fitting that on February 2, 1974, the Feast of the Presentation of the Lord, when the Holy Year in Rome was still in its infancy, all of Pope Paul's teachings on Mary were summed up by him in a splendid document, the apostolic exhortation *Marialis Cultus.*

It is easy to make the simple observation that this exhortation on devotion to the Blessed Virgin is a tripartite document, involving (1) the place of Marian devotion in the reformed liturgy—the Roman calendar, the Roman Missal and Lectionary, the Breviary, and other liturgical books and actions; (2) directives on pastoral and theological orientations for the authentic magisterial renewal of Marian devotion; and (3) suggestions on the Angelus and the rosary.

It is far from easy, however, to do justice to the profundity and the uniquely balanced character of this presentation of authentic magisterial teaching. There is just no way, other than careful reading, rereading, and meditation, for us to make this teaching our own.

Le me give a few examples of Pope Paul's unique insights:

> Every authentic development of Christian worship is necessarily followed by a fitting increase of veneration for the Mother of the Lord.

> The Church's reflection today on the mystery of Christ and on her own nature has led her to find at the root of the former and as a culmination of the latter the same figure of a woman: the Virgin Mary. . . . [Hence the Church's] adoring respect for the wise plan of God, who has placed within His family (the Church), as in every home, the figure of a woman, who in a hidden manner and in a spirit of service watches over that "family" and carefully looks after it until the glorious day of the Lord.

> Mary is *the Attentive Virgin* . . . Mary is also *the Virgin in Prayer* . . . Mary is also *the Virgin-Mother.* . . . The ancient fathers rightly taught that the Church prolongs in the Sacrament of Baptism the virginal motherhood of Mary. . . . Mary is, finally, *the Virgin presenting offerings* . . . a mystery of salvation that in its various aspects orients the episode of the Presentation in the temple to the salvific event of the Cross.

> Mary is, above all, the example of that worship that consists in making one's life an offering to God. . . . Mary's "yes" is for all Christians a lesson and example of obedience to the will of the Father, which is the way and means of one's own sanctification.

> It is supremely fitting that exercises of piety directed

toward the Virgin Mary should clearly express the Trinitarian and Christological note that is intrinsic and essential to them. . . . They [exercises of piety] . . . should clearly show also the place she occupies in the Church . . . both the Church and Mary collaborate to give birth to the Mystical Body of Christ . . . thus love for the Church will become love for Mary and vice versa.

Mary, the new woman, stands at the side of Christ, the new Man, within whose mystery the mystery of man alone finds true light; she is given to us as a pledge and guarantee that God's plan in Christ for the salvation of the whole man has already achieved realization in a creature: *in her.*

I have no doubt that with this apostolic exhortation Pope Paul has gone a long way toward fulfilling the second part of Don Bosco's prophecy, which had spoken of chaos following an ecumenical council in the next century. But, he said: "Once the Holy Father has succeeded in anchoring the barque of Peter between the twin columns of devotion to the Blessed Sacrament and Our Lady, the storm will subside and a great period of triumph for the Church will supervene."

10. The Pope and the Eucharist

We have adverted to Pope Paul's preoccupation with the Second Vatican Council, from the very beginning of his pontificate to the present, and with the benefit of hindsight we can understand his preoccupation.

His very first encyclical letter was *Ecclesiam Suam*, issued while the council was in full stride, so to speak, and before his approval and ratification of the pivotal document of the council, the dogmatic constitution on the Church, *Lumen Gentium*. In the encyclical he was at pains to state that he was deliberately refraining from passing any judgment of his own on doctrinal points concerning the Church which were under examination by the council, so that the latter would have full liberty of study and discussion. He did say, however, that "in virtue of our office of teacher and pastor, and placed at the head of the Church of God, we reserve to ourself the choice of the proper moment and manner of expressing our judgment. *We are most happy if we can present it in perfect accord with that of the Conciliar Fathers.*" In other words, he was not about to rubber-stamp any document. Then he specified in summary fashion the essential truths about the Church, with copious reference to the scriptural sources and the teachings of the fathers, doctors and saints of the

Church, and those of his predecessors in the chair of Peter.

The first of these truths, which virtually includes all the others, is *the vital bond of union of the Church with Christ*, the doctrine of the mystical body of Christ. As Pope Pius XII wrote, "We first learned of the Mystical Body of Christ, which is the Church, from the lips of the Redeemer Himself" (*Mystici Corporis*, 1943). And Pope Paul took as his own the exhortation of his predecessor in that same encyclical on the mystical body: "We must accustom ourselves to see Christ in the Church. It is Christ who lives in the Church, who teaches, governs and sanctifies through it. It is Christ, too, who manifests Himself differently in different members of His society." Renewal, *aggiornamento*, in Pope Paul's view, is inseparable from this fundamental truth.

> Let us repeat it once again for our common admonition and profit. The Church will rediscover her renewed youthfulness not so much by changing her exterior laws as by interiorly assimilating her true spirit of obedience to Christ and accordingly by observing those laws which the Church prescribes for herself with the intention of following Christ. Here is the secret of her renewal, here her *metanoia,* here her exercise of perfection.

It is apparent from a comparison of this encyclical with the council's document on the Church that the latter benefited greatly from Pope Paul's guidance in the encyclical. But we are concerned here with a different aspect of the letter. It foreshadows, as it were, the treatment of the Blessed Mother that would characterize the council's teachings about her.

Having based reform and renewal and updating on the perennial doctrine of the mystical body and the outpouring of charity that must flow from it, Pope Paul said, "This vision of humble and profound Christian perfection leads our thoughts to Mary Most Holy, for she reflects this vision most perfectly and wonderfully in herself; she lived it on earth, and now in Heaven she rejoices in its glory and beatitude. . . . *We regard devotion to Mary as a source of Gospel teaching.*"

It is not surprising, then, to find that Pope Paul's efforts to promulgate and clarify the council's teachings on the

Church have proceeded along twin paths, namely, instruction about and renewal of devotion to our divine Lord and his blessed Mother.

It is very evident, both from the encyclical *Ecclesiam Suam* and the dogmatic constitution on the Church, that the theological foundation of all valid ecclesiology is Christologic. The Church is the continuation of the incarnation in time. As St. Augustine put it, *"He and we are the Complete Man."* This is the mystery of the Church, to which Pope Paul keeps turning his attention and ours, again and again. But as he said, "The mystery of the Church is not a mere object of theological knowledge—it is something to be lived!" So it is most fitting that he should immediately turn to her who alone has lived that mystery to the full. In the words of St. John Bosco's prophecy, the Holy Father has sought to anchor the barque of Peter to the column that is the Blessed Virgin, so that its mooring to the other column, our Lord in the blessed Eucharist, will be easier and more secure.

We alluded to the fact that the second encyclical he issued was on our Lady, and in our last chapter we considered the scope of Pope Paul's teachings about her and his incessant appeals for renewed devotion to her. The ink was scarcely dry on that encyclical when he was at work on the third, which was given in Rome on September 3, 1965, and titled *Mysterium Fidei*. The title was, of course, most appropriate since it was on the holy Eucharist. The date of issuance, September 3, was also most appropriate, for it was the Feast of Pope St. Pius X, immortalized by the title "the Pope of the Eucharist."

This encyclical is the best place to begin our consideration of Pope Paul's teachings on the Blessed Sacrament since it does two things: it reaffirms the age-old teachings of the Church and identifies the erroneous theological opinions concerning the Eucharist, and, secondly, it pleads powerfully for renewed devotion to our Lord in the Blessed Sacrament, so that the hope "that a new era of Eucharistic piety [may] pervade the whole Church" may be fulfilled. This is evident from the descriptive official title, *Concerning the Teaching and Worship of the Most Holy Eucharist*. It is emphasized very strongly and almost immediately by the Holy Father, as he based the encyclical on defined truth.

> In order to make evident the indissoluble bond which exists between faith and devotion, the Fathers of the Council [Vatican II], *confirming the doctrine which the Church has always held and taught, and which the Council of Trent solemnly defined,* decided to prefix to their treatise on the Most Holy Mystery of the Eucharist the following summary of truths: *"At the Last Supper, on the night when He was handed over, Our Savior instituted the Eucharistic Sacrifice of His Body and Blood, to perpetuate the Sacrifice of the Cross throughout the ages until He shall come, and so entrusted to the Church, His Beloved Spouse, the memorial of His Death and Resurrection; a sacrament of devotion, a sign of unity, a bond of charity, a paschal banquet in which Christ is received, the soul is filled with grace and there is given to us the pledge of future glory."* [Constitution on the Sacred Liturgy, ch. 2, no. 47]

A marvelously concise and inclusive summary, giving the historical data, the theological essentials of the dual nature of the Eucharist as sacrifice and sacrament, its ecclesiologic character, and its immediate as well as its eschatological relation, meaning, and effect for the individual follower of Christ, no less than for the entire Church. The Holy Father commented: "In these words are emphasized both the Sacrifice, which pertains to the essence of the Mass which is celebrated daily, and the Sacrament."

Then, after expressing his hopes that "rich fruits of Eucharistic devotion will grow from the restored Sacred Liturgy," he spelled out some of the major doctrinal errors that, despite the council document, were being spread abroad.

1. Putting such emphasis on the "communal" Mass as to disparage Masses celebrated in private.
2. Overemphasizing the symbolic or sacramental aspects of the Eucharist so as to overshadow the real presence and the sacrificial nature of the action; for example, emphasizing the Eucharist as a meal, as a memorial, as a social function, rather than as the supreme reenactment of redemptive divine love and the ultimate in worship.
3. Misinterpreting the mystery of transubstantiation as defined by the Council of Trent, rendering it as "tran-

signification" or "transfinalization," thus emptying the doctrine of its real meaning.

4. Denying the doctrine of the *continuing* real presence of our Lord in the Blessed Sacrament, that is, in the consecrated hosts which are left after Mass has ended.

Pope Paul's response to these errors is to set forth once more the essential truths about the Eucharist, against the background of two fundamental and necessary propositions. In the first place, *the Eucharist is a very great mystery*; in fact, *it is the mystery of faith*, "to which many illustrious martyrs have borne witness with their blood, which celebrated Fathers and Doctors of the Church constantly professed and taught," and in which alone, as Pope Leo XIII remarked, "are contained, in a remarkable richness and variety of miracles, all supernatural realities" (*Mirae Caritatis*).

The second proposition follows inevitably from the first: "*We must therefore approach this mystery with humble obedience, not following human arguments, which ought to be silent, and adhere firmly to Divine Revelation.*"

The pope appealed to striking statements of such fathers of the Church as St. John Chrysostom, St. Cyril, St. Thomas, and St. Bonaventure in support of these propositions, but above all he referred to the supreme court of appeal, our blessed Lord himself, recalling the reaction of many disciples to his words about the absolute necessity of eating his flesh and drinking his blood and the Lord's response to their disbelief. The story is told in St. John's gospel (6:61–69), but we would do well to meditate on it again and try to realize its meaning.

We tend, with the hindsight of faith, to be rather critical of those disciples (many in number, as we read) who incredulously muttered, "This is a hard saying, who can listen to it?" and turned away and left him. But let us put ourselves in their place, if we can. Would it not have sounded like an incredible or offensive and outrageous statement even if we had (as they must have) listened to the other teachings of our Lord that *did* make sense, and had seen him work miracles, such as the multiplication of the loaves and fishes, with which he had fed the multitude but a day or so earlier?

"*This is a hard saying, who can listen to it?*" How often has not this exclamation, or its equivalent, been uttered by men since that day! How often is it not found in the speeches and writings of theologians throughout the history of the Church! Do we not hear it today, also, among the learned ones?

The only response possible was made by Peter, speaking for the apostles and for us all, when our Lord, so far from mitigating or watering down or restating his incredible words, turned to the twelve and asked, "Will you also go away?" Peter promptly answered, "*Lord, to whom shall we go? Thou hast the words of eternal life.*" As it was then, so it is now, and will be to the end of time.

We must then, as a logical conclusion, the pope asserted, "follow as a guiding star in our investigations of this mystery, the Magisterium of the Church. . . . *But this is not enough. Having safeguarded the integrity of the faith, it is necessary to safeguard also its proper mode of expression,* lest by the careless use of words, we occasion (God forbid) the rise of false opinions regarding faith in the most sublime of mysteries. . . .

> *The norm, therefore, of speaking which the Church,* after centuries of toil and under the protection of the Holy Spirit, *has established and confirmed by the authority of Councils,* and which has become more than once the watchword and standard of correct belief, *is to be religiously preserved, and let no one at his own good pleasure or under the pretext of new science presume to change it. . . . We are not to tolerate anyone who on his own authority wishes to modify the formulae in which the Council of Trent sets forth the Mystery of the Eucharist for our belief.* For by these formulae . . . concepts are expressed which are not tied to one specific form of human civilization, nor definite period of scientific progress, nor one school of theological thought, but they present what the human mind by universal and necessary experience grasps of realities and expresses in suitable and accurate terminology, taken either from the language commonly in use or from polished diction. *For this reason, these formulae are adapted to men of all times and all places.*

So much for the new theology and its tired errors! *Habemus papam!* We have a pope; and he, no less than his predecessors on the throne of Peter, is the hammer of heretics.

He set forth thereafter "for the edification and joy of all," he said, "the doctrine which has been handed down concerning the Mystery of the Eucharist and which the Catholic Church holds and unanimously teaches." This doctrine is the anvil on which the hammer of Peter is to be used to bend our Modernist heretics back into shape. *But it is for us also an anvil on which we must shape our entire lives into that image of God in which we were created. It is the means, the only means, by which we may become one with Christ, our brother and Lord.*

The following is a summary of the main and essential doctrinal points discussed by Pope Paul in the rest of the encyclical, with copious reference to and quotations from Scripture and the fathers and councils of the Church.

1. The very essence of the doctrine is that *the Mass, the holy Eucharist, is a sacrifice*—a marvelous reenactment of the Sacrifice of the Cross, and *by its means the saving power of the latter is constantly recalled and applied for the forgiveness of sins.*

2. As Moses sanctified the Old Testament with the blood of calves, our Lord, by instituting the mystery of the Eucharist, sanctified the New Testament with his own blood: "This Cup is the New Covenant in My Blood, which shall be shed for you."

3. This mystical reenactment of Calvary was for all time and all places: "Do this," he said, "in memory of Me." In a word, it was to be universal, in time and place. And from the earliest days it was so. As St. Luke recorded, "They continued steadfastly in the teaching of the Apostles and in the communion of the breaking of the bread, and in the prayers" (Acts 2:42).

4. Foreshadowed by Malachias, this new sacrifice of the New Testament has always been offered by the Church, in accordance with the teaching of our Lord and the apostles, "not only to atone for the sins and punishment of the living faithful and to appeal for their other needs, but also to help those who have died in Christ but have not yet been completely purified" (Conc.

Trident., *Decret. de Ss. Miss. Sacrif.*, ch. 2).

5. *It is the entire Church which,* in union with Christ functioning as priest and victim, *offers the sacrifice of the Mass* and is *offered in it* (since the Church is the mystical body of Christ). This was taught by the fathers of the Church, for example, St. Augustine (*City of God*, X:6), it was explained in recent years by Pope Pius XII (*Med. Dei*), and finally the Second Vatican Council repeated it in its treatise on the people of God in the constitution on the Church.

6. *This teaching,* which is the most effective means of fostering devotion to the Mass and extols the dignity of all the faithful, *must not and does not blur the distinction between the universal priesthood of the faithful and the ministerial or hierarchical priesthood, which is a distinction of essence and not merely one of degree* (*L.G.*, 2:10).

7. Every Mass, even though a priest may offer it in private, is not something private; it is an act of Christ and of the Church.

8. *In the sacrifice of the Mass Christ is made sacramentally present.* This means, first and foremost, that *the Eucharist is both sacrifice and sacrament.* As Pope Paul put it, "Both sacrifice and sacrament pertain inseparably to the same mystery and one cannot be separated from the other. The Lord is immolated in an unbloody manner in the Sacrifice of the Mass . . . when by the words of Consecration He begins to be *sacramentally present.*"

What is meant by those words, "sacramentally present"? The pope reminds us that Christ is present in his Church in many ways—when she prays, when she performs works of mercy, when she preaches the word, when she rules and governs the people of God, when she administers the other sacraments—all of these are signs of Christ's presence. He is present in a manner most sublime when the Church worships —when she offers the sacrifice of the Mass in his name. How does this presence differ from every other presence? We know it does, *for it is called the Real Presence.* This does not imply that all those other types of presence are not real, but only that it is *presence in the fullest sense, because it is a substantial presence of the whole and complete Christ, God and man.*

The Eucharist then, as sacrifice and sacrament, is not only a symbol, though symbol it is of unity and charity in the Church, but *a real and substantial personal presence.* Pope Paul aptly quoted the words of Theodore of Mopsuestia, who said, "The Lord did not say, 'This is a symbol of My Body, and this is a symbol of My Blood,' but *'This is My Body and My Blood' "* (in *Matt. Comment*, C. 26, P.G. 66, 714).

> 9. *Christ our Lord is present in the sacrament of the Eucharist by transubstantiation.*

This term "transubstantiation" has been a stumbling block for many, and still is. It is, it is true, a clumsy, manufactured, or synthetic word, the kind Aristophanes called *epe hamaxiaia* ("charioted" words); but it is no more so than those that Modernist theologians and their heretical predecessors have sought to substitute for it, such as "transsignification" and "transfinalization." Pope Paul deals simply and masterfully with these aberrations:

> To avoid misunderstanding this sacramental presence . . . we must listen with docility to the voice of the teaching and praying Church. *This voice, which constantly echoes the voice of Christ, assures us that the way Christ is made present in this Sacrament is none other than by the change of the whole substance of the bread into His Body, and of the whole substance of the wine into His Blood, and that this unique and truly wonderful change the Catholic Church rightly calls transubstantiation.*

Then he added: "After transubstantiation has taken place, the species of bread and wine undoubtedly take on *a new meaning* and *a new finality*." In other words, "transsignification" and "transfinalization" are correct terms, *so far as they go.* This of course is true of many if not all heresies—they express or contain a partial truth.

"However," Pope Paul continued, *"the reason they take on this new significance and this new finality is simply because they contain a new 'reality'* which we may justly term on-tological . . . and that *not only because of the faith of the Church, but in objective reality.* . . . Nothing remains of the bread and wine but only the appearances under which Christ, whole and entire, in His physical reality is bodily present." In a word, he is here!

> 10. Since this is so, and Pope Paul quotes many fathers of the Church, the councils, and his predecessors as witnesses to the unchanging faith of the Church in the matter, the Church has always offered, and still offers, the cult of *latria*, the worship which may be given to God alone, to the sacrament of the Eucharist, not only during Mass but also outside of it, reserving consecrated Hosts with the utmost care, exposing them to the solemn veneration of the faithful, and carrying them in processions.

This faith and practice has been in the Church from the beginning. It gave rise to the Feast of Corpus Christi and, in later times, to eucharistic congresses, national and international. And our Holy Father earnestly exhorts us (in the closing paragraphs of this encyclical) to return to ever greater faith and devotion to our Lord in the Eucharist, to daily Mass, to daily Communion (recalling and quoting the decree of Pope St. Pius X in 1905), and to frequent visits to the Blessed Sacrament.

It remains only to consider some of the other words and actions whereby Pope Paul reaffirmed, since the issuance of this fundamentally important encyclical, his profound faith and his devotion to the mystery of the Eucharist.

In August 1968 he left Rome for Bogotá, Columbia, to attend the International Eucharistic Congress there. The day before his departure he spoke to his audience about the meaning and purpose of eucharistic congresses. He recalled that they had begun only in the last century, prompted by a saintly French woman, Martha Tamisier, and that the organization of eucharistic congresses had been approved by Pope Leo XIII in 1881. "As you know," he said, "the Eucharist synthesizes our religion: a doctrinal synthesis because

It is a continuation of the Incarnation of the Word of God among us, and a sacramental renewal of the sacrifice of Christ; *all of revelation is concentrated in this focal point*, the most mysterious and luminous of our faith." "The resounding mysteries which God works in silence," in the words of St. Ignatius of Antioch.

But why a congress? For one thing, the pope sees, reflected in the great display of homage that a eucharistic congress offers, "the gesture of Mary at Bethany when she broke the sealed vase of alabaster and poured the precious, perfumed unguent on the feet and hair of the Savior. . . . Thus understood, a Eucharistic Congress is not an act of rhetorical triumph, but rather a contemplative act fulfilled by the ecclestical community."

In the context of South America, the pope believed the congress must unite all its participants in Christ and with one another. He obviously had no illusions about the material poverty he expected to see, and the stirrings of impatience and rebellion even in the clergy. But the solution to deplorable conditions of life, he asserted, is neither reactionary revolution nor recourse to violence—*it is love*. "*Not rhetorical and weak love, but that which Christ in the Eucharist teaches us—love which gives of itself, which multiplies itself, which sacrifices itself.*"

Pope Paul took up this theme of love on June 2, 1969, in reflecting on the forthcoming feasts of Corpus Christi and the Sacred Heart. "What is the discovery that the faithful make," he asked, "on seeking the complete and deep sense of Divine Revelation? *The discovery is love. God revealed Himself mainly in love.* The whole history of salvation is love. The whole Gospel. . . . *The story of Christ is summed up in St. Paul's famous synthesis: 'I live by faith in the Son of God, Who loved me and gave Himself up for me' (Gal. 2:20).*"

How absolutely right the Holy Father is! Eighteen simple Anglo-Saxon words sum up the good news of the gospel and the proper response of the Christian. "I live by faith in the Son of God, Who loved me and gave Himself up for me."

"Beloved Sons," the pope concluded, "do you know this? Do you think of it? How do you intend to respond?"

There is no doubt whatsoever about the response Pope Paul had in mind. If we believe in the Son of God, we must believe all he has taught—*all*, without prevarication or exception. That summary synthesis of St. Paul was expanded into a wealth of teaching in his many epistles; it has been expanded and developed over the centuries by the teaching Church. There is no doubt that one of the most fundamental teachings, a stumbling block to many still, after nearly 2,000 years—but a sure touchstone of the authenticity and reality of our profession of faith in the Son of God-made-man—is this very doctrine of the Eucharist.

Listen to Pope Paul on May 26, 1970, as he says: "The Lord does not allow doubtings, nor does He permit elusive exegesis of the authentic reality of His words as given in the texts. *He made it a matter of confidence!*"

The pope, giving a homily at the Holy Thursday Mass in his own cathedral church, St. John Lateran, continued:

> So this is a decisive hour, the hour of faith in which Jesus' words are wholly accepted, even though they be incomprehensible. . . . Two notes rise above the rest. . . . *They are the notes of love and death.* . . . Everything is concentrated in the sacramental action which has just been recorded: *Body and blood — love and death, and one word is enough to express them. It is sacrifice!* . . . It is the heart and sum of Christian life. It is the mandate, the memorial, the passion, the charity of Christ being transfused into His Church, into us, so that we may live from Him and for Him, offer ourselves up in sacrifice also for the salvation of the world, and, one day, rise with Him again.

There can be no doubt what our response to the marvelous gift of the Eucharist must be: the response invited by him who is really and truly present on our altars, and echoed and re-echoed by his vicar on earth. *It is sacrifice!* If we do not participate willingly and lovingly in the redemptive sacrifice of our blessed Lord, we will *not* avoid suffering. But our suffering will be meaningless, useless, wasted.

When misfortunes and sufferings come upon us, we had better remind ourselves of Don Bosco's words:

> What does Our Lord do in the Blessed Sacrament? Endlessly He prays to His Eternal Father on our behalf, and

withholds the chastisements that our sins deserve. If nowadays we do not see or hear of such frightful punishments as once befell the Jewish people, *it is not because our sins are fewer* or less outrageous! You are aware that today has its evil men too! Who is it that unceasingly holds back Divine justice every day, every moment?
None other than Our Lord Jesus Christ!
In the Sacrifice of the Mass He again offers Himself for us as a Victim upon our altars. *At the sight of His Sacred Wounds, the destroying angel sheathes his sword.*

"And so," our Holy Father said on the eve of Corpus Christi in 1972, "the feast [of Corpus Christi] is, therefore, a rethinking of that fact and that mystery. . . . This is what we wish to tell you. . . . *The Eucharist is for us*, pilgrims on earth bound for Heaven, *the focal point, blinding and illuminating, of the whole real system of our Christian religion.* It is the presence of Emmanuel, that is, 'God with us,' Who is redemption, a Divine Victim for us, in a word, a plan of Divine communion in us. The more impenetrable, the more unusual, the more miraculous the Eucharistic Mystery appears to our worldly way of thinking, the more clear, logical, persuasive and beatifying It is to the man who believes in and who loves Jesus Christ."

11. The Humanism of Pope Paul

Let us be precise about the meaning and significance of this topic. Do we mean to say that Pope Paul is a humanist, a secular humanist, as the terms are used nowadays? God forbid! As always, there is need to define and understand the terms of our discourse; so a little preliminary exposition of the etymology and historical development of the meaning of a few words is in order.

The word "secular" is first found in Middle English, between the mid-twelfth century and the end of the fifteenth. It derived from the Latin *saeculum*, meaning an age or generation. But by the time it made its way into Middle English usage, directly or indirectly from Old French, it had two meanings. It was

1. Related more closely to the classical Latin original: "of or belonging to an age or long period."
2. Obviously colored by Vulgate Latin usage: "of or pertaining to the world," hence "worldly," and also "nonecclesiastical," "non-religious," "nonsacred."

By contrast, the term "secularism" did not appear in English usage until 1846, when, full blown like Athene from the brow of Zeus, it was introduced to refer to "the doctrine that morality should be based solely on regard to the well-being of mankind in the present life, to the exclusion of all considerations drawn from belief in God or in a future state."

The words "human," "humanist," "humanism" had a similar history. The parent word, "human," derived from the Latin *humanus*, was rendered into Middle English as "humane" (humayn[e]) and was not differentiated from the term "humane" until the early eighteenth century. At that time, "human" and "humayn" (Middle English) had the same meaning, namely, "of, belonging to, or characteristic of man," but as early as 1533 the word "humane" was also used to mean "mundane," "secular," "opposed to divine."

The word "humanist" had been in English since 1589, when it meant "one versed in the humanities," "a classical scholar." But by 1617 it also had acquired the meaning "a student of human affairs or of human nature."

When the term "humanism" was first introduced in 1812, it still referred to "the quality of being human," "being devoted to human interests," but by 1860 it was used to refer to "any system of thought or action which is concerned with merely human interests." And although it was applied in 1876 to describe the philosophy of Auguste Comte, logical positivism, it came to be synonymous with "the religion of humanity."

Nowadays it is common to speak of *"secular humanism."* This is, in a way, tautological, since, as we have seen, "secularism" in 1846 and "humanism" in 1860 had come to refer to the same thing—"religion without God, the religion of humanity." And now, as anyone knows who has read the humanist manifesto, secular humanism is an anti-God religion, an even worse contradiction in terms!

Also, "humanism" was used by Samuel Taylor Coleridge, in a sense now obsolete, to refer to "belief in the mere humanity of Christ." This belief and its corollary, disbelief in the divinity of our blessed Lord, are at the heart of the Modernist heresy, now ravaging the Church again in full fury.

Against this background, how can we speak of the humanism of Pope Paul? We can let him speak for himself. As we have come to appreciate in our discussions of the teachings of the

Holy Father, there is no shortage of material. Week after week, year after year, there has been and there continues to be an outpouring of instruction, of exhortation, on every topic related to the life of man, the life of the Church, and divinely revealed truth.

But there is no doubt, in my mind, that the year 1968 witnessed the high point of the exposition and clarification of true humanism, Christian humanism, the humanism of the council and of Pope Paul VI. On July 17 of that year he spoke to a general audience of "the question, now occupying our own thought, regarding human perfection, the ideal toward which modern man ought to aim." He reviewed, quickly and in bold strokes, the mentality of modern man, the iconoclast, rejecting the past *in toto*. "Everything has to be given a new concept . . . everything has been mistaken . . . what is wanted is a new humanism, so new indeed that they are continually rejecting the humanist formulas put forward yesterday, or even today."

He sees this restless search, however, as a great opportunity, "especially in the favored environment of our ecclesial community." The reason is clear:

> The whole of the teaching on the perfection of Christian living, the destiny of holiness that emerges from the very call to follow Christ, the affirmation of the values not only of the supernatural sphere of grace but of those also of the temporal order and of natural activities, spread throughout its documents by the Council, strengthens our belief that the follower of Christ still can have and *ought to have a moral grandeur* — inherited from the past it is true, but *alive and meant to be lived, a grandeur of which . . . he has the secret, the true formula, in the doctrinal field.*

This is Pope Paul's formulation of the key truth about theology—the inseparable relation between moral theology and dogmatic theology. St. Thomas had the same truth in mind when he raised, at the very outset of his *Summa Theologia*, the fundamental question about sacred doctrine: *Is it merely speculative, or also practical?* The answer was characteristic—lucid and matter of fact: "Whereas some among the philosophical sciences are theoretical and others are practical, *sacra doctrina* takes over both functions" (1, 1, 4).

It is my conviction that a major share of the blame for the sorry state of Catholic moral theology in modern times can be laid to *ignorance,* or *ignoring* the essential and inseparable connection between moral and dogmatic theology, between the moral law and the defined truths of the faith. How else explain the arrogant dissent from the Church's constant moral teaching on such fundamental matters as sexual behavior, abortion, social justice, and so on—dissent "justified" on the grounds the Church has never defined as *de fide* any of her moral teachings? What nonsense! *The Church does not need to define moral doctrine*—it is *implicitly* contained in the defined doctrines of the faith, *and cannot be separated from them without violence and death.* No wonder the Holy Father spoke of that moral grandeur which the follower of Christ must have: "Alive and meant to be lived . . . of which . . . he has the secret, the true formula, in the doctrinal field."

"The Christian," he declared, "if he really is one, *is the true man,* he *is the man who realizes himself fully and freely,* and he does this by modeling himself on an example of infinite perfection and of unsurpassed humanity, Christ Our Lord, who can be imitated *in those necessary ways required by faith and grace."*

He directly confronted the objection, often recurring in history and widespread today, that the Catholic religion, especially in its presentation of moral teaching, degrades the moral sense, putting dogmatic doctrine before the dictates of conscience. He referred to Manzoni's refutation of this objection, and his own observations provide an excellent summary of the essentials of Christian humanism.

He *defended the relation between religion and morality:*

> We maintain, in accordance with all the theological and teaching tradition of Christianity, *that grace perfects nature;* that is to say that the faith, religious living, reference of our activity to God as to its beginning and end, the example and virtue that come from the Gospel, instruction given to the faithful by the Church . . . the practice of prayer and of the fear of God . . . *these do not deform man's character, do not degrade his liberty, do not displace the inner workings of his conscience.* Still less do they authorize the believer to evade his obligations in the natural and civil sphere, or turn him into a bigoted and

hypocritical pharisee. No! *They strengthen in a man the true sense of manhood. . . .* The believer need not fear he will be the last or even the second at the winning post of that human ideal with which the contemporary mentality is concerned.

In the concept of the perfect Christian great importance must be attached to the moral virtues proper to human nature considered as a whole — sincerity, veracity . . . justice, both commutative and social, the sense of duty, courage, magnanimity, honesty in habits, and so on.

We must appreciate these natural virtues highly, even though not forgetting that, outside the order of grace, they are incomplete and often are linked up with very deplorable human weaknesses — above all we remember that *of themselves they are unproductive of supernatural value.*

So, he said, quoting relevant passages from the document on the Church in the modern world (*Gaudium et Spes*, 30 and 36), the council

puts before the Christian a wise humanism which . . . *raises the Christian to the stature of the complete man,* to the fullness of the gifts received, together with life itself, from God, to the ordered balance of his faculties, to the unwearied and harmonious employment of his powers, to the community sense in his own actual human relationships, to the dignity of his own conscience, not certainly as *the* criterion of free and responsible moral conduct. It is good that . . . the Church of God speaks to each and all of perfection, *the human moral perfection of everyday life.*

But is this all? There are many voices crying out "Yes, this *is* all!" There are so many for whom *Gaudium et Spes* is the seminal document of the Second Vatican Council, indeed the only one worth reading or attending to, since it puts man where he belongs—center stage. Is this the humanism of Pope Paul?

The very next week, on July 24, 1968, at his general audience, he returned to the fray.

What is man? What type of man can we call the ideal? The ancient Socratic question is back again: "I ask you — What is a holy man?" (Plato, *Eutifrone*).

We put the question . . . to bring into present relief a difficulty arising from our own profession of "theocentricity" — the central position which God occupies in the Christian conception of life, as against the modern self-idolatry or "anthropocentricity" — the humanistic and profane concept of man which puts him at the center of everything.

We are talking rather of the penitential way of life which stands at the very threshold of participation in the Kingdom of Heaven. . . . This way of life calls for renunciations . . . a sense of sin . . . watchfulness . . . an imitation of Christ which is far from easy . . . even to the exaltation of His cross and some measure of share in His sacrifice . . . abnegation, mortification, penance . . . *Christianity has no trust in naturalistic humanism.* It knows that man is an entity wounded from his very beginning . . . bearing within himself a lack of balance that is extremely dangerous and needs austere and lasting discipline. . . . The Christian life is not soft or easy. It is not comfortable and a matter of form. It is not blindly optimistic, morally accommodating and spineless. *It is joyous but it is not happy-go-lucky!*

In a word, it is most adverse, indeed anathema, to the modern mentality, which aims at a full, comfortable, spontaneous, happy-go-lucky sort of life. How often have we not heard the very comments quoted by the Holy Father!

It [the modern mentality] considers the Christian to be inhibited and scrupulous, excluded from the greatest experiences, which are usually those of unrestricted passion, outside the strong currents of fashionable broadmindedness whether in thought or in conduct. . . .

We cannot forget the words of the Master, commenting on the accident that happened when the tower of Siloe fell and caused the death of eighteen persons — "Except you do penance, you shall all likewise perish" (Luke 13: 4-5). And this keynote of repentance . . . of penance and reparation, is sounded throughout the Gospel . . . *Christian penance is for the new man, the perfect man.* It is functional; it is not an end in itself. It does not lessen a man; it is an art whereby he is restored to his primeval likeness, that which reflects the image of God and which God had in mind when He created man (Gen. 1:26-27). *It is an art whereby, after the afflictions of penance, there is imprinted on the countenance of man the paschal splendor of the Risen Christ. That is our humanism!* . . . "He who hath ears to hear, let him hear" (Mark 4:23; Matt. 19:12).

On the day following this general audience address, namely, July 25, Pope Paul published his encyclical *Humanae Vitae.* What can we say about this superlative document, which tells us more than any other about authentic Christian humanism, the humanism of Pope Paul VI?

We are all aware of the reception it received, from the vociferous, arrogant, and scandalous dissent of some theologians and their followers to the quiet, prayerful gratitude of countless Catholic priests and laity and the splendid and spirited endorsement of Malcolm Muggeridge. All that is history, though the repercussions are still with us and will be for a long time.

We could not hope to do justice to such a sublime and epochal encyclical in this chapter. Let us simply try to see how it fits with what we have reviewed of the humanism of Pope Paul. The very title is most revealing—*Humanae Vitae.* It is concerning human life that the pope writes, not just contraception. He makes this very clear in the second section of the encyclical, dealing with doctrinal principles, where he stated:

> The problem of birth, *like every other problem regarding human life, is to be considered,* beyond partial perspectives — whether of the biological or psychological, demographic or sociological orders — *in the light of an integral vision of man and of his vocation, not only his natural and earthly, but also his supernatural and eternal vocation.*

Two things are immediately evident. First, in Pope Paul's view (and that of any thinking person), regulation of birth cannot be dealt with in isolation but must be put in the perspective of the whole human being, not only the natural man but man called to a supernatural life. Second, problem solving in the moral sphere of man's total life must be accomplished in the light of God's revealed truth.

Hence the Holy Father proceeds to establish the *doctrinal* foundation for the *moral* teaching he wished to reaffirm and elaborate later in the encyclical. This foundation, he asserted, is the true concept of the two great realities of married life, namely, *conjugal love* and "responsible parenthood."

Concerning the former he wrote, "Conjugal love reveals its true nature and nobility when it is considered in its supreme origin, God, Who is love, 'the Father from Whom every family in Heaven and on earth is named.' " Hence the characteristic marks and demands of conjugal love: "It is first of all *fully human,* that is to say, of the senses and of the spirit *at the same time* . . . it is *total* . . . it is *faithful* and *exclusive* until death. . . . And finally this love is *fecund*, since it is not exhausted by communion between husband and wife, but is destined to continue, raising up new lives."

Responsible parenthood can be rightly understood only in the light of these characteristic marks and demands, and Pope Paul's exposition is brief and to the point. However, I wish to underline two statements, chiefly because they have been ignored or vigorously denied, at least in part.

"In relation to physical, economic, psychological and social conditions," said the Holy Father, "responsible parenthood is exercised *either by the deliberate and generous decision to raise a large family, or by the decision, made for grave motives and with due respect for the moral law, to avoid for the time being, or even for an indeterminate period, a new birth.*" Such a definition of responsible parenthood is of course anathema to the secular humanists, especially the statement that having a large family could be an exercise of responsible parenthood. How many Catholics have swallowed, uncritically, the equation responsible parenthood = zero population growth?

The pope continued: "Responsible parenthood also and *above all* implies a more profound relationship to the objective moral order established by God, of which a *right* conscience is the faithful interpreter . . . in the task of transmitting life; therefore, *they are not free to proceed completely at will,* as if they could determine in a wholly autonomous way the honest path to follow; *but they must conform their activity to the creative intention of God, expressed in the very nature of marriage and of its acts, and manifested by the constant teaching of the Church.*"

In the remainder of the encyclical the Holy Father spelled out that same constant teaching. And, as remarked previously, it brought down upon him the instant opprobrium and invective of those who apparently had convinced themselves that he would approve and ratify *their* consensus.

As if anticipating the storm soon to burst upon him, Pope Paul spoke to his general audience on July 31, 1968, just a few days after publication of the encyclical. He gave, as it were, an advance *apologia pro opus suum*—a moving and frank account of his labors, his feelings, his fears, his hopes and convictions about the matter.

> The first feeling was that of a very grave responsibility [he said, which sustained him in his efforts but which also oppressed him]. We confide to you that this feeling caused us much spiritual suffering. *Never before have we felt so heavily, as in this situation, the burden of our office. . . .* How often have we felt almost overwhelmed by the mass of documentation! How many times, humanly speaking, have we felt the inadequacy of our poor person to cope with the formidable apostolic obligation of having to make a pronouncement on this matter! . . .
>
> After imploring the light of the Holy Spirit, we placed our conscience at the free and full disposal of the voice of truth. We sought to interpret the Divine Law that flows from the very nature of genuine human love, from the essential structure of married life, from the personal dignity of husband and wife, from their mission of service to life, as well as from the sanctity of Christian marriage. We reflected on the firm principles of the traditional doctrine in force in the Church, and especially on the teaching of the recent Council. We pondered over the consequences of one or other decision, *and we had no doubt about our duty to give our decision in the terms expressed in the present encyclical.*

The "one or other decision" over which he agonized was, of course, what he referred to earlier as "the alternatives of *an easy condescension to current opinions,*" powerfully reinforced by the majority recommendation of the commission instituted by Pope John and enlarged by himself, or "*of a decision that modern society would find difficult to accept.*"

Thank God, the Holy Spirit of truth prevailed and once again Peter confirmed the faith of his brethren. And with faith, a feeling of hope stirred in the heart of the supreme pontiff:

> We hoped it would be well received for its own intrinsic merit and for its humane truth, notwithstanding the widespread difference of opinion today. . . . We hoped that scholars, especially, would be able to discover in the document the genuine thread that connects it with the Christian concept of life and which permits us to make our own the words of St. Paul: *"But we have the mind of Christ"* (1 Cor. 2:16).

But alas, so many Catholic "scholars" discovered nothing

in it other than confirmation of their preconceived notion that nothing good had ever come out of Rome except mindless suppression of human freedom.

The vicar of Christ, however, steadfastly and repeatedly puts forward the authentic view of man and his *essential* freedom, not the freedom espoused by Hegel, which would make man more than God, who cannot choose evil, but rather the freedom of the sons of God, a freedom that the pope asserted (on September 4, 1968) derives from the fact of man's "creaturehood," made in the image of God, the creator, whereby he is "elevated into the ineffable love of Christian regeneration and raised to the level of son and of participant in the divine nature." Truly a Christian humanism, the only hope for man, if he wishes to fulfill himself as a person and as a social being.

"Only the law and grace of Christ can offer this to man," our Holy Father maintains, *"not as a Utopia but as a reality, not as a suppression of individual personality but as a broadening and an exaltation of it, in that supreme design known to us as the Communion of Saints."*

On October 16 that same year, the pope focused once more on the question of human freedom. He spoke of "the apologia of freedom, in its various aspects of personal freedom . . . the exigency of human dignity . . . freedom of the Sons of God proclaimed by the Gospel . . . freedom of conversion . . . freedom in the Church . . . religious freedom within civil regimes . . . freedom of scientific research . . . freedom of information, of association," etc.

All these freedoms, he said, we find suffused throughout the council documents. *What is the answer to this clamor for freedom on all sides?* The pope gives it in one word, a word that has all the force and decisiveness of a sharp sword, or a machete, clearing away the undergrowth of verbiage that has grown up and all but choked the concept of freedom. The word is *obedience,* a word no longer tolerated in modern conversation, he observes, even where of necessity the reality survives. The real world, however, bears witness to the necessary link between obedience and true freedom, because where the ancient civil and Christian virtue of obedience is radically negated, totalitarian tyranny flourishes—the totalitarianism of ideas imposed by the mass media and the conformism and oppression enforced by the police state. So, the pontiff declares, the whole plan of our salvation depends on a free and responsible exercise of obedience.

What is this obedience that generates peace, *obedientia et pax*, in the formula beloved by Pope John XXIII? "It is," according to Pope Paul, "the mystery of obedience in Christ Our Lord, a mystery radiating from the whole Gospel, a mystery that our Savior defines, and a mystery in which we participate." So he exhorted his audience, and us, speaking above the tomb of St. Peter and using Peter's exhortation to the first Christians: "At the revelation of Jesus Christ, be as obedient children" (1 Pet. 1:13–14).

We can say, therefore, without equivocation or fear of contradiction, that true humanism in the mind of Pope Paul consists in obedience to the law of Christ and of his Church, and imitation of him who is the way, the truth, and the life.

"Without Christ there is no true humanism," cried the Holy Father on Christmas Day 1969. "We implore God and beg you, men of our time, to spare yourselves the fateful experience of a Christ-less humanism. . . . Human virtues, developed without the Christian charism, can degenerate into their contradictory vices. Man, making himself a giant without a spiritual, Christian animation, collapses under his own weight. . . . *Man on his own does not know who he is. He lacks the authentic prototype of humanity*; he creates idols for himself, idols that are fragile and sometimes dishonorable. *He lacks the true Son of Man, the Son of God: a living model for the true man.*"

This is the constant yardstick by which the Holy Father measures man's desires, ambitions, reflections on his own nature, and his moral actions. God incarnate, God redeeming in Jesus Christ, his Son our Lord, risen from the dead and seated in the glory of his Father. There we find the true measure of man.

On May 12, 1971, the Holy Father made some very profound comments on the characteristic aspect of the Risen

Christ. He spoke of

> His living and real corporeity — His real body — but
> an incorruptible, immortal, glorious body. . . .
> Does this transformation . . . of the Lord's human body
> not mean something to us in relation to the initiated assi-
> milation of our lives with His? . . . The Church and her
> faithful sons know that the Resurrection of the Lord,
> reflected in us by the celebration of the Paschal Mystery,
> offers and teaches us, nay rather asks of us a new con-
> ception, a new elevation, a new sanctification of our body.
> In more common terms, a new purity. Yes, Easter must
> give us a new sense of the dignity of this flesh of ours, so
> sensitive and frail. *It is the work of God. It is the temple
> of the Holy Spirit.*

In the light of this doctrinal affirmation, which is the
ground for authentic humanism, and only in its light, we can
appreciate the moral teachings of the pope, of the supreme
magisterium, whether it be in *Casti Connubii, Humanae Vitae,* the declaration on procured abortion, the document on
contraceptive sterilization, or that on sexual ethics, not to
mention the entire corpus of magisterial teachings on social
and commutative justice.

We have come almost full circle in our discussion of the
teachings of Pope Paul VI. At the outset we questioned, with
him, what it means to be a Christian and the seriousness of
our claim to be Catholics. Focusing in this last chapter on
the humanism of Pope Paul has, I hope, stirred up in us
again the implications of the faith we have and hold. It is
a faith that, in the practical order, demands that we accept
and live up to, so far as we can, *all* the teachings of the
Church. For she is the Bride of Christ, our Savior, and
speaks to us in his name through Peter and his successors. If
we find some of these teachings hard, we can only say with
Peter: "Lord, to whom shall we go? Thou hast the words
of eternal life, and we have come to believe and to know that
Thou art the Christ, the Son of God" (Jn. 6:69–70).

Bibliography

Aquinas, Saint Thomas. *Summa Theologiae*. Book One, 1265-1274, edited by Thomas Gilby, O.P., et al. New York: McGraw Hill, 1963.

Augustine, Saint. *De Fide Et Symbolismo*. Library of Christian Classics, edited by John Burnaby. vol. 8. Philadelphia: Westminster Press, 1955.

Chesterton, G. K. *Christendom in Dublin*. London: Sheed and Ward, 1932.

Eusebius. *Historica Ecclesiae*. Minneapolis: Augsburg Press, 1963.

Flannery, Austin, O.P., ed. *Vatican Council II / The Conciliar and Post Conciliar Documents*. Northport, N.Y.: Costello Publishing Company, 1975.

Hughes, Philip. *The Church in Crisis: A History of the General Councils, 325 - 1870 (Vol. 2)*. Westminster: Christian Classics, 1963.

Lewis, C. S. *Mere Christianity*. New York: Macmillan, 1964.

Manzoni, Alexander. *The Betrothed*. Translated by Archibald Colquhoun. New York: Dutton, 1951.

Newman, John Henry. *The Development of Christian Doctrine*. New York: Doubleday Image Books, 1960.

Ott, Ludwig. *Fundamentals of Catholic Dogma*. Cork: Mercier Press, 1957.

Pope Paul's apostolic exhortations, encyclicals and Credo of the People of God are the official English translations as reprinted by the publications division, United States Catholic Conference, 1312 Massachusetts Avenue, N.W., Washington, D.C. 20005.

Pope Paul's addresses, to general audiences and special groups, and his homilies are as given in "The Pope Speaks" for 1968 through 1973 issued by the publications division, United States Catholic Conference, (address listed above).

Sheed, F. J. *To Know Christ Jesus*. Westminster: Christian Classics, 1963.

Theodore of Mopsuestia. *In Matt. Comment*. Edited by Greca Patrol. Vol. 66, pp. 705 ff. J. P. Migne Publishing, 1864.